micro macramé basics & beyond

knotted jewelry with beads

macramé basics & beyond

knotted jewelry
with beads

Raquel Cruz

KALMBACH BOOKS

Kalmbach Books
21027 Crossroads Circle
Waukesha, Wisconsin 53186
www.Kalmbach.com/Books

Published in 2014
18 17 16 15 14   1 2 3 4 5

Manufactured in the United States of America

ISBN: 978-1-62700-046-8
EISBN: 978-1-62700-169-4

Editor: Erica Swanson
Art Director: Lisa Bergman
Photographers: William Zuback, James Forbes

Library of Congress Control Number: 2014942403

Contents

introduction

A new passion awaits

Whether you are a micro-macramé hobbyist or a professional artist in this emerging craft, you'll find a project in this book that fits you perfectly. Although the knots used in macramé have been in use for a long time, as a designer, I bring a new look to this favorite pastime. It's my goal to revive your passion for macramé or, if you've never done any knotting, introduce a delightful new obsession to you. Along the way, I will share new techniques and valuable tips that get great results and may save you some time.

The fine knotting cord used in micro macramé produces tiny, refined-looking knots that are beautiful and colorful when used in jewelry. Cord for micro-macramé is easy to find in any of your favorite colors. Add beads from your stash or the bead store, and your micro macramé becomes a lovely bracelet, necklace, or other accessory.

The first part of the book teaches you basic knots, terminology, and techniques. Projects start easy, and then become more involved as you sharpen your skills. The projects in the final chapter introduce a few specialty knotting techniques.

Adapt these techniques to your designs and your favorite colors, and the possibilities for creativity will become endless.

Raquel

basics
getting started

Materials & tools

Cord

0.5mm nylon cord: All of the projects in this book are made with this size. Here are a few different brands:
- C-Lon beading cord
- #18 S-Lon from the BeadSmith
- #5 Tuff Bead Cord from Eurotool
- Conso Nylon #18, available as 170-yd. spools

Beads

Crystals and pearls: You can use almost any bead with a hole larger than 0.5mm. Try Swarovski crystal beads and large-hole Swarovski crystal pearls. Czech glass beads—even in the smaller size (3mm)—fit the 0.5mm cord well.

Seed beads: Try 6º, 8º, and 11º glass seed beads in several shapes—teardrops, rocailles, Miyuki Delica, and Toho (the last two have larger holes than other seed beads). I recommend that you avoid color-lined and metal-lined seed beads, as the stringed cords will remove the color inside the hole of the bead. Also, avoid dyed beads because the coat often is not permanent. With metal seed beads, the hole is slightly larger than the hole in other seed beads.

Other beads: Stone chip beads, Czech glass buttons, oval and round cabochons, and stones that can be mounted in a knotted bezel all work well in micro-macramé.

Findings

Clasps: Almost any kind of clasp can be used to fasten this jewelry. Choose from toggle clasps, hook-and-eye clasps, lobster clasps, box clasps, multi-strand clasps, domed end caps, cones, or buttons.

Cord ends: Select fold-over crimp ends with loops or cord-end glue-ins.

Cord end beads: Use these for the braided ends. I like large metal seed beads or small round beads.

Jump rings: 4mm jump rings are great for extension chains and connecting clasps.

Split rings: I use these to mount the cords at the beginning and at the end of a project, which will be fastened with a lobster or similar clasp.

Tools

Knotting board: Make your own or buy one (see next page).

Pins: I use size 22 and size 20 sewing pins only.

Masking tape: This keeps the ends of the cords out of the way.

Tape measure, ruler, scissors, and pliers (flatnose, roundnose): Use these tools to measure, cut, add the findings to the pieces, and also to pull the embroidery needle through the knots.

Wire cutters: The sharp point of these jewelry cutters allows you to trim cord ends really close to the work.

Crewel embroidery needle: Use these needles in different sizes to undo misplaced knots and to help pass cord ends through knots to finish them.

Hairstyling flat iron: Straighten unruly cords with an old flat iron. (Do not iron the tips of the cords because this will flatten them and the seed beads will not fit.)

Kumihimo disk: Although I don't include instructions on how to use it in this book, this disk is very easy to handle and can be used to add braided ends to pieces.

Fray check: Typically the cords used in micro macramé are fairly stiff, but after stringing many beads, the cords tend to soften. I recommend using a liquid sealant on the cord ends, especially if you are stringing a large number of seed beads.

Using a knotting board and pins

The ideal surface for macramé is firm and accepts pins to hold your work in place.

Commercial knotting board: I recommend the BeadSmith macramé board, which comes in two sizes: 10x14" (25x35.5cm) and 6x9" (15x23cm). These boards have measurements on the face and slits around the entire board similar to a foam kumihimo disk. The rigid surface allows the slits to firmly hold the cords and also allows for the use of pins, if necessary. I like the small size because my pieces are usually small and the notches are close.

DIY knotting board: I made my own board from a 15x18" wooden cork board, layered with a several sheets of craft foam, covered with fabric, and stapled on the backside. I use the board slightly inclined. I made several washable slipcovers, and a gardener's kneeling pad makes a notched edge on the bottom to hold the working cords in order.

> When I first unwrapped my purchased board, it had a strong odor. Wait a few days before using the board; the odor should completely go away.

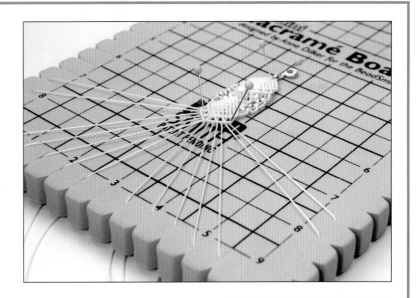

How to place pins:
• Before pinning a cord end to the board, make a slip knot and pin it by the knot so the cord doesn't split.
• Slanting the pins, place them against the direction from which you are pulling the cords. If you change the direction of the knotting constantly or need extra stability, place two pins leaning in opposite directions.
• If the cord end is too short to make a slip knot, use a piece of masking tape over it; this is a temporary solution that can be used to hold cords in place.
• Keep pinning the piece down as you work to ensure the knots are neat.

Which glue when?

• Use superglue for an instant bond. Don't use superglue if the glued part is going to touch your skin, as it hardens the tips of the cord.
• Use fabric glue, such as Aleene's Fabric Fusion glue pen, because it dries clear, is flexible, and doesn't scrape skin.
• Use E6000 adhesive to glue the knotted piece to a metal component. Clean the tip of the tube after each use to prevent the lid from sticking.

Basic knotting techniques & terms

There are only a few basic knots for macramé. Repetitions and combinations of these knots make other composite knots that are sometimes recognized by their own names.

Abbreviations

LHk: lark's head knot

DHHk: double half-hitch knot

THHk: triple half-hitch knot

Hk: half knot

SQk: square knot (or flat knot)

Cord Vocabulary

The cords' names can change according to their functions.

Holding cord: This cord holds the knots. A cord is recognized as the holding cord when it is the base where the other cords are attached while a project is started (also known as the *mounting cord*). A holding cord also holds the knots that are wrapping around it by other cord or cords. For this case, the cord may be called the *anchoring cord*.

Knotting cord: This cord is used to make the knots around a holding cord.

Runner cord: When making multiple lines of horizontal and/ or vertical double half-hitch knots, this cord goes from left to right and vice versa.

Filler cord (or core cord): This is one or more cords in the center of a square knot.

Floating cord: This cord is placed apart from the cords being worked because it will not be used in one or more rows. Tape or pin it as needed.

LARK'S HEAD KNOT (LHk)

The lark's head knot and some of its variations are usually used to mount the cords at the beginning of a project. It can also be used to increase the number of cords later in a project, increase the width of a project, or create a loop for a clasp.

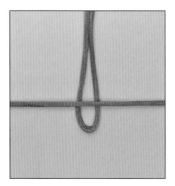

Fold the cord in half. With the ends toward the top, place the loop underneath the mounting cord.

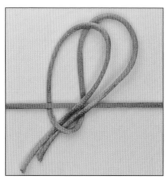

Pass the two ends over the mounting cord and through the loop.

Pull the ends to the bottom to tighten.

Reverse Lark's Head Knot

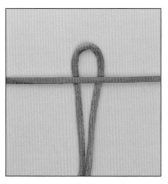

Fold the cord in half, place the loop underneath the mounting cord with the ends toward the bottom.

Bring the two ends through the loop.

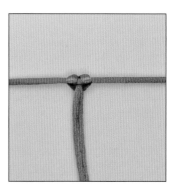

Pulling the ends to the bottom to tighten.

Reverse Lark's Head Knot with Half-Hitch

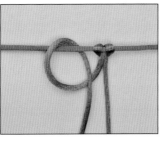 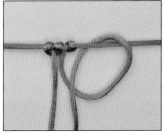 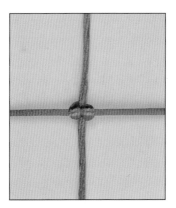

Start out with a reverse lark's head knot.

With each end of the cord, go around the mounting cord from the front, and pull the end through the loop.

Vertical Lark's Head Knot and Lark's Head Knot Chain

Starting with two cords, take one cord as the knotting cord and the other one as the holding cord. Pass the knotting cord over and around the holding cord, passing the end between the loop formed by the two cords. Pull the knot into place.

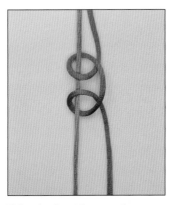 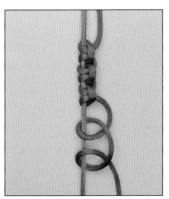

Take the knotting cord under and around the holding cord, slipping the end between the loop formed by the two cords. Pull the knot into place.

The repetition of previous steps will create a lark's head knot chain.

HALF-HITCH

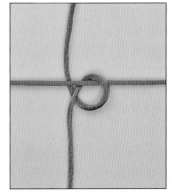

The half-hitch is one of the two basic knots in macramé. It is made of one loop around a holding cord. It is usually tied twice, resulting in the double half-hitch knot (DHHk).

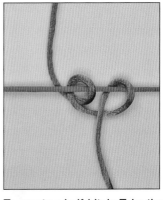 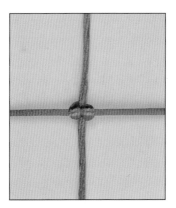

To create a half-hitch: Take the knotting cord end under and over the holding cord, and then go behind the knotting cord. Repeat once for a DHHk, twice for a triple half-hitch knot (THHk), and so on. The DHHk can be knotted in a horizontal, diagonal, or vertical direction.

Horizontal Double Half-Hitch Knot

Choose one cord to be the holding cord, and place it over the other strands (knotting cords) in a horizontal position.

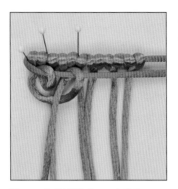 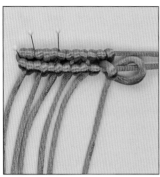 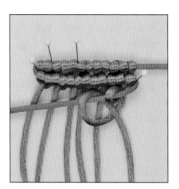 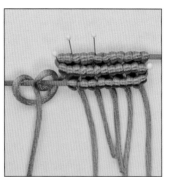

To work DHHk from left to right: Using the first knotting cord, wrap over and around the holding cord, passing the end between the loop formed by the two cords. Tighten the loop by maintaining the holding cord taut horizontally. This is the first half-hitch. Repeat a second time with the same cord to complete the DHHk.

Repeat the previous step with the next knotting cords.

You can also work DHHk from right to left.

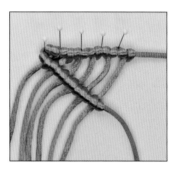

When the holding cord is held downwards, a diagonal DHHk is formed.

Vertical Double Half-Hitch Knot

This knot uses the same knotting cord to create double half-hitch knots over the vertical cords, which are the holding cords. Before making each knot, place the knotting cord under the holding cord.

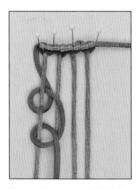 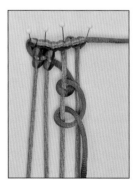 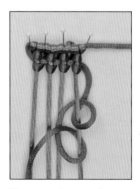 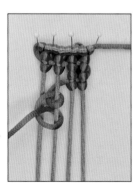 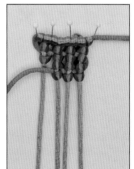

To work vertical DHHk from left to right: Grab the holding cord taut while tying the DHHk with the knotting cord. Adjust the knot.

Bring the knotting cord under the next holding cord and continue as before until the row is completed.

You can also work vertical DHHk from right to left as shown.

Alternating Half-Hitch Chain

For a chain, use one cord as the knotting cord and make a half-hitch on the other cord. Alternate the cords, so one time one cord will be the knotting cord, and next time, the same cord will be the holding cord.

Alternating Double Half-Hitch Chain

This chain is created by tying a sequence of one left-sided DHHk and one right-sided DHHk. There are two ways to recognize whether the DHHk is left-sided or right-sided. First, note which side the small ridge formed by the knot is facing; second, note which side the knotting cord is ending. This will tell you if the knot is left or right sided. Start with one or more holding cords and one knotting cord.

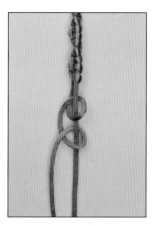

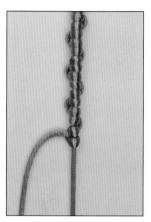

Using the knotting cord, tie a left-sided (or right-sided) DHHk over the holding cord.

Bring the knotting cord to the opposite side under the holding cord, and tie a right-sided (or left-sided) DHHk.

HALF KNOT

Half knot is the second basic knot in macramé. It is usually made of three or more cords. The two outer cords are the knotting cords, while the inner cords are known as the filler cords. The filler cords should be held taut.

Left Half Knot

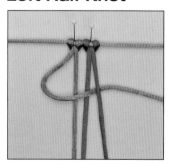
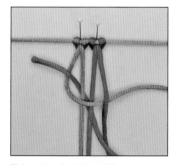
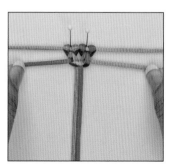

Bring the left knotting cord over the filler cords, forming a "four" shape.

Take the right knotting cord and bring it over the left knotting cord, under both filler cords, and pull its end up through the loop that was formed by the left knotting cord.

Tighten the knotting cords. Repeating left half knots results in a spiral rope.

Right Half Knot

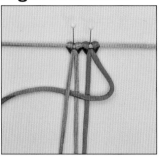

Place the right knotting cord over the filler cords, forming an inverted "four" shape.

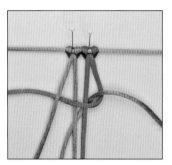

Take the left knotting cord and bring it over the right knotting cord and under both filler cords, and pull its end up through the loop that was formed by the right knotting cord.

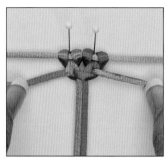

Pull the knotting cords tight. Repeating right half-knots results in a spiral rope.

SQUARE KNOT (SQk)

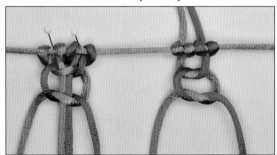

If you forget which side you worked last while working on a chain of square knots, look for the last bump that has formed on the sides. The cord on this side is the one you should fold over the filler cords next.

Also known as flat knot, the square knot is made of one left half knot and one right half knot. The filler cords are held taut until the knot is completed. The SQk can also be made without the filler cords.

OTHER KNOTS AND TECHNIQUES

Accumulating Knots

Start with the first cord as the holding cord and let multiple cords hang vertically. The hanging cords will be the knotting cords first, and then each one will become one of the holding cords. This knot is usually used to bring all of the cords to one side. Accumulating knots can be tied in a horizontal or diagonal direction.

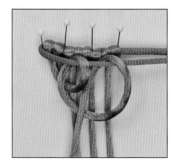

Tie a DHHk over the holding cord.

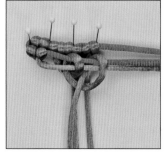

Add the knotting cord to the holding cord and tie a DHHk over the holding cords (now there are two holding cords).

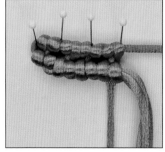

This step keeps repeating, while the holding cords increase in number to form a bundle.

Slip Knot

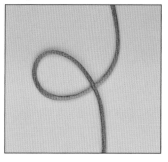 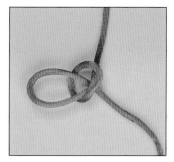

Form a loop, placing the short end on top of the loop, then under the loop. Grabbing part of this short end through the loop, pull and form another loop. Do not let the end come through. Tighten.

Overhand Knot

Take a cord and make a loop. Take one end over and pass it through the loop formed. Pull the ends to tighten.

Adding a new cord

If, despite all your careful calculations, you run out of cord, you can add extra cords to the work. In my experience, the best place to add a new cord is between a horizontal or vertical row of DHHk.

If you run out of the knotting cord in a vertical or horizontal DHHk row: Place the short end of the cord to be replaced behind the work. Add the new cord, leaving a tail, with a DHHk over the holding cord. Secure the ends of the old and newly added cords behind the piece by passing the ends through some of the knots on the back. Continue the work using the new cord.

If you run out of the holding or runner cord in a DHHk row: Place the new cord behind the piece and where you need to add it. Tie the next knot over the old cord and the newly added cord together. Make a few more knots over these two cords, then release the old cord and continue using the new one only. If you are using beads, you can add a cord within the hole of the bead, knot the old and new cord, and cover the knot with the bead.

When your piece is done, apply glue over these knots and cut the excess cords. Plan ahead if you are adding more than one cord. Do not add all of them at the same time. Add one, then a few rows below another, and so on.

Estimating cord length

This is the most common way to calculate the cords' lengths: Every end should be four times longer than the piece being made. This length should be doubled when the cord is mounted by folding it in half. However, this can vary widely, depending on the function that each cord plays, the kind of knots and the pattern being made, how tight or loose every person knots, the diameter of the cords, etc.

The best way to calculate the approximate length is by making samples. I use my leftover cords in different colors to make these. I write down the length I start with; this way, I can compare these with the length I have left over. Also, I keep a

record as a reference for future projects. Using a cord of 0.5mm in diameter, I found out that one DHHk uses approximately ½" (13mm) of cord. When making a DHHk or another similar chain, every 1" (2.5cm) of chain will use approximately 10" (25cm) of cord.

After all the calculations, I always give the cords an extra length (10"/25cm) to work comfortably. If in doubt, cut more than you think you will need. For holding cords, this length can be close to the finished length of your jewelry, plus a few inches to end the piece.

Crossing Two Cords

Cross two cords to tie DHHk over them. **[FIG 1]**. Identify the left and right cords you want to cross. Make a slip knot at the end of the cord that crosses over from the right side. Pin it close to the cord in the left side. Now, taking the crossed cords as the holding cords together, make the DHHk through the loop formed by the right, holding the cord from left to right. Release the slip knot you made before on the end of the right cord. Pull and adjust both holding cords. If the right cord twists as you pull, place a pin in the loop that is formed. Continue pulling and moving the pin even closer to the work until the loop disappears.

If you are crossing the cords to make the last row of DHHk in the work, before pulling the loop through completely, apply a dot of superglue on a portion of the cord that will go inside the DHHk row. Don't spread the glue over the cord; just let the small drop of glue sit while you pull the cords all the way through. Let it dry and clip both holding cords as close as possible to the sides.

Passive Knotting Cord

Passive knotting is useful when you are working with a very long knotting cord (for example, if you are making several rows of DHHk with a single knotting cord or a chain that uses the knotting cord a lot). Also, if you have beads strung onto the knotting cord, they make it difficult to knot in a normal way because the beads and the slip knot made to secure the beads gets stuck as you wrap. So instead of wrapping with the knotting cord, make a loop on it, then pass the holding cord through the loop.

Left-Sided DHHk

Loop the long end of the knotting cord up and over itself as shown **[a]**. The loop should be facing the holding cord, with its end facing the opposite side (left). Use your index finger and your thumb to keep the loop closed as you pass the holding cord through the loop from the front to the back **[b]**. Keeping the holding cord taut, adjust the knot by pulling the knotting cord. A half-hitch has now been formed **[c]**. Repeat in the exact same way to complete the knot **[d, e]**.

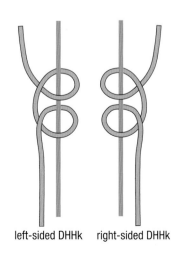

left-sided DHHk   right-sided DHHk

FIG 1

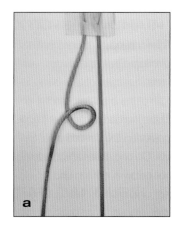

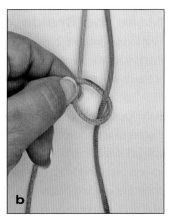

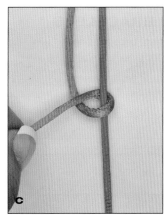

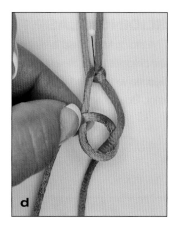

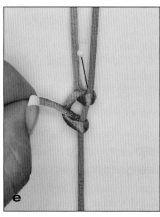

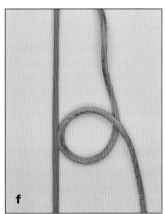

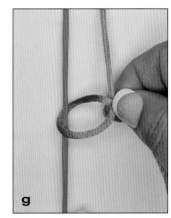

Right-Sided DHHk

Make a loop with the knotting cord placing its long end up and over itself as shown **[f]**. The loop should face the holding cord and its end should face the opposite way (right). Use your index finger and your thumb to keep the loop closed as you pass the holding cord through the loop, from the front to the back **[g]**. Keeping the holding cord taut, adjust the knot by pulling the knotting cord. You just have created a half-hitch **[h]**. Repeat in the same way to complete the knot **[i, j]**.

Vertical LHk

Although both loops in this knot should face the same side, the second loop is formed in a slightly different way from the first. Make a right-sided vertical LHk. Tie the first half-hitch of this knot, making the loop and passing the holding cord through it in the exact same way as the DHHk (in this case, the right-sided DHHk). Make the second loop, placing the long end of the knotting cord *under* itself. Use your index finger and your thumb to keep the loop closed as you pass the holding cord through the loop, *from the back to the front*. Keeping the holding cord taut, adjust the knot by pulling the knotting cord. The left-sided vertical LHk is made by inverting the position of the holding and knotting cords and forming the loops toward the right.

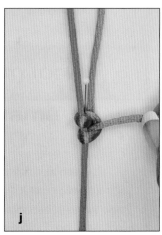

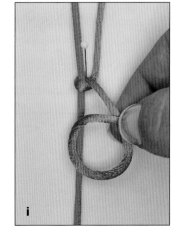

projects
fast & easy

Delicious Arm Candy *Bracelets*

Knot this graceful set of bracelets while you learn and practice some of the most basic knots in macramé. The use of multicolor cords, three bright and three light in this case, adds interest, but at the same time provides unlimited possibilities. Whether you are combining the same colors in different ways, adding other colors, or simply using different color combinations, have fun playing with the patterns.

MATERIALS & TOOLS
- fabric glue
- superglue
- fray check
- embroidery needle
- flatnose pliers
- scissors
- macramé board and pins

Zigzag Bracelet
- **7** 40" (1m) cords 0.5mm nylon cord, in different colors
- **2** 6mm end beads or cord ends
- 1g 11º seed beads in each of **3** colors

Zigzags and Spirals Bracelet
- 0.5mm nylon cord
  80" (2.03m) color A
  50" (1.27m) each of colors B and C
- 3g 8º metal seed beads
- **2** 2x3mm crimp tubes
- **2** 4mm fold-over crimps with loop
- **2** 4mm jump rings
- extender chain
- lobster claw clasp

Alternating Curves Bracelet
- 0.5mm nylon cords
  110" (2.8m) color A
  30" (76cm) each of colors A and B
- **2** 2x3mm crimp tubes
- **2** 4mm fold-over crimps with loop
- **2** 4mm jump rings
- extender chain for bracelet
- lobster clasp

Framing Beads with Square Knots Bracelet
- 0.5mm nylon cords
  2 15" (38cm)
  2 20" (51cm)
- assortment of glass beads, 6mm rondelle spacer beads, and metal seed beads
- **2** 6mm glass end beads

Rondelles and Twists Bracelet
- 0.5mm nylon cords
  2 15" (38cm)
  2 40" (1m)
- **3** 6x8mm faceted rondelle glass beads
- **2** 6mm rondelle spacer beads
- **2** 8º metal seed beads
- **3** 6mm metal end beads

Material notes
Use 0.5mm nylon cord, such as C-Lon beading cord, in different colors. Make sure the beads' holes are wide enough to fit the cords at least two times. The end beads should fit 4–6 cords.

Zigzags and Spirals Bracelet:
Color A is the knotting cord for the spiraled pattern. You will use colors B and C for the zigzag pattern.

Alternating Curves Bracelet:
Use the color A (110"/2.8m) cord as the knotting cord to tie the alternating DHHk chain.

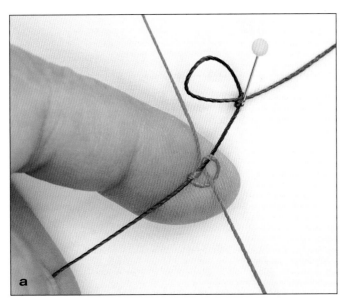

a

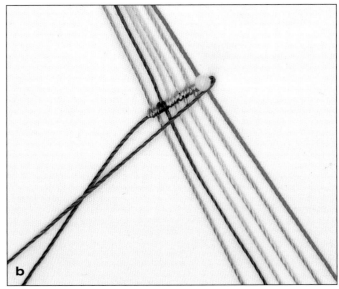

b

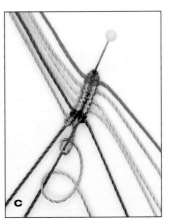

c

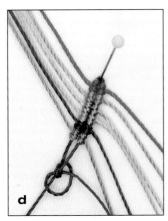

d

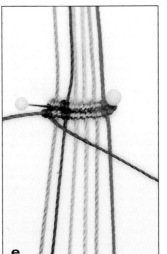

e

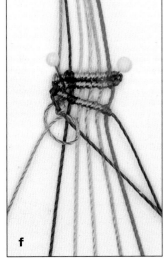

f

Zigzag Bracelet

1 Choose one of the cords to be the holding cord. Apply fray check to 1" (2.5cm) of the ends, and let it dry completely. Clip off the tips diagonally.

2 Tie a slip knot in the middle of this cord, and pin the knot to the board.

3 Leaving a 7" (18cm) tail, attach one of the remaining cords below the slip knot with a double half-hitch knot (DHHk). Keep the cord in place by holding it between your index finger and thumb while you create the DHHk with your other hand **[a]**. Add the five other cords in the same way.

4 Release the slip knot made on the holding cord, bring that end to the left side, and use it as the holding cord **[b]**. Pull both ends to the same length, and make a second row of DHHk with all the cords to the left, including the other end of the holding cord **[c, d]**.

5 Place and pin the piece horizontally. Starting from the left, use the second cord as the holding cord to tie a diagonal row of DHHk with each of the next six cords **[e]**. Create another row of diagonal DHHk, using the first cord to the left as the holding cord **[f]**. You have two holding cords, both on the right-hand side.

6 String three 11º seed beads on the holding cord that is further out **[g]**.

7 Place a pin close to the inner holding cord. Holding the cord on a diagonal angle, tie a row of DHHk using the six cords to the left. Using the exterior holding cord, make a second diagonal row beneath this row **[h]**.

8 Once both holding cords are on the left side, repeat step 7, knotting in the opposite direction (from left to right). Start knotting over the inner holding cord **[i]**.

9 Repeat steps 6–8 until you have 1" (2.5cm) less than the desired wrist size.

10 Make the two last rows: Use the outer holding cord as the knotting cord to tie a DHHk over the inner holding cord **[j]**. This knotting cord became a holding cord again to make a *horizontal* row of DHHk in the direction of the rest of the strands **[k]**. After that, the holding cords will be on opposite sides **[l]**. The separation between the previous row of DHHk and this row will be shorter.

11 Cross the two holding cords to make a second row of DHHk over them, using the six hanging cords, from left to right **[FIG 1]**: On the end of the cord that crosses over from the right side, make a slip knot. Pin it close to the holding cord on the left side. Taking the crossed cords together as the holding cords, make the DHHk through the loop formed by the

right holding cord, from left to right. Do not adjust the knots too much.

12 Next, release the slip knot from the end of the right cord. Pull both holding cords to get rid of the loop **[m]**. If the cords' loop twists as you pull, place a pin in the center of the loop and continue pulling and moving the pin even closer to the work until you have a small loop **[n]**. Before pulling the loop completely through, place a dot of superglue on a portion of the cord that will go inside the DHHk row. Don't spread the glue over the cord; let the small drop of glue sit while you pull the cords through. Let it dry, and clip both holding cords close to the sides.

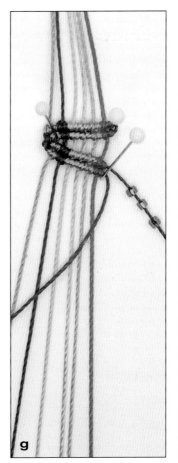

g

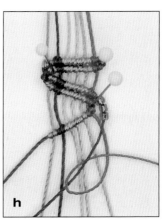

h

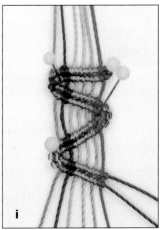

i

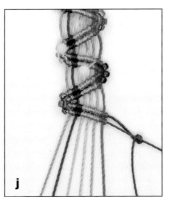

j

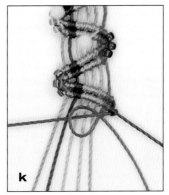

k

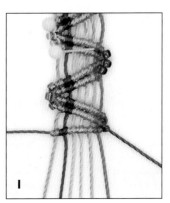

l

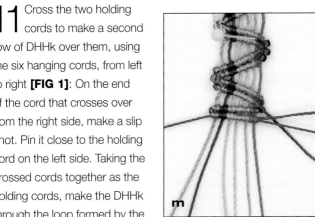

m

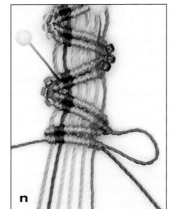

n

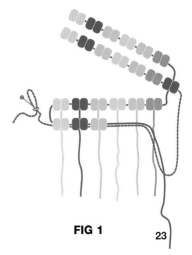

FIG 1

23

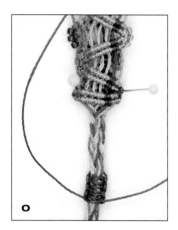

o

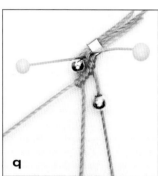

q

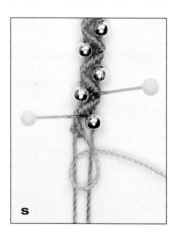

s

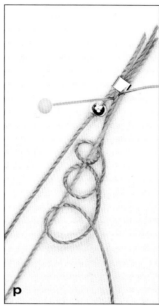

p

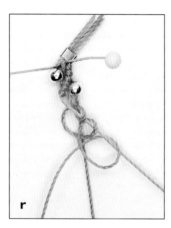

r

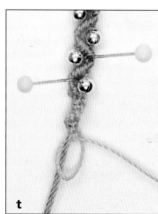

t

13 Braid the cords' ends and make a sliding knot clasp (Basics, p. 18) **[o]**.

Zigzags and Spirals Bracelet

This bracelet wraps around the wrist twice and is made of two segments equal in length.

> You can also make shorter segments with the two different patterns.

Secure the Ends

1 To begin, hold the three cords together and thread one crimp tube onto one end. Leaving about a 1" (2.5cm) tail, arrange the cords in a flat position. Note that the longer cord (color A) is placed to the right; the other two can be placed in any order. For extra security, apply a small amount of superglue inside the tube.

2 Next, use flatnose pliers to squeeze the crimp tube. The longer cord will be the *runner cord* for the first pattern of this bracelet and the knotting cord for the second pattern.

First Pattern

3 Pin the cords onto the board, and string an 8º metal seed bead on the left cord. Pick up the runner cord as the holding cord, and tie a triple half-hitch knot (THHk) with each of the cords to the left **[p]**.

4 String an 8º seed bead on the right cord **[q]**. Using the same cord (cord A) as the holding cord, tie a THHk with each cord to the right **[r]**. If you want to have sharp corners, place a pin at the beginning of each row.

5 Repeat steps 3 and 4 until you reach the desired length. Leave the runner cord in the middle.

Second Pattern

6 Now the runner cord will be the knotting cord to make a chain of right- (or left-) sided half-hitches until you reach the desired length **[s, t]**.

> While working on this chain, the half-hitches and the knotting cord will rotate toward the opposite side. This makes it difficult to keep working normally. What works for me is to make seven half-hitches at a time; next, I bring the knotting cord under the holding cords to bring it to the correct place again. Repeat as desired.

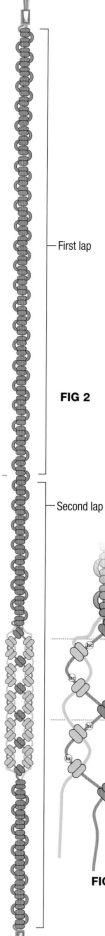

First lap

FIG 2

Second lap

FIG 3

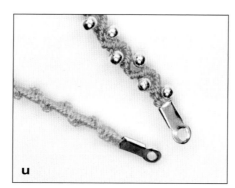

u

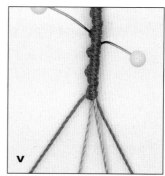

v

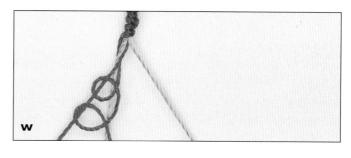

w

Finish

7 String another crimp tube on the cords, placing it as close to the knots as possible.

8 Apply a drop of superglue and flatten the crimp tube as in step 1. Trim the excess cords on both ends of the bracelet.

9 Cover the crimp tubes with the fold-over crimps, placing the folding sides on the back of the bracelet [u].

10 Add a split ring and an extension chain to one end and a split ring and a lobster claw clasp to the other end.

Alternating Curves Bracelet

This bracelet wraps around the wrist twice. It is made by knotting alternating DHHks, with one 2" (5cm) curved pattern inserted in the center or any part of the second lap you want [FIG 2].

1 Start this piece as in the Zigzags and Spirals Bracelet, but string four cords instead of three on the crimp tube. Place the color A cords on the edges.

First Pattern

2 Using the longer color A cord as the knotting cord, tie a chain of alternating DHHk over the rest of the cords until you reach the appropriate length [v].

> It is easy to forget which side of the alternating DHHk chain you have knotted last. When this happens, look for the last ridge the knotting cord has formed, and point the knotting cord toward that side to make the next DHHk.

Second Pattern

3 Switch the cords so the color A cords are in the middle.

4 Tie one DHHk with the two central cords (color A) [w]. Number the cords from 1–4. Use cord 2 as the holding cord and cord 1 as the knotting cord to tie two alternating DHHk, starting with a right-sided DHHk

and then a left-sided DHHk [FIG 3]. The knotting cord should end toward the left.

5 Repeat step 4 on the right side in the opposite direction: Taking cord 3 as the holding cord and cord 4 as the knotting cord, make two alternating DHHk starting with a left-sided and then a right-sided DHHk. Your knotting cord should end toward the right.

6 Finish and join the first motif, using the holding cords in the middle to create a DHHk. Tie the knot in the same direction as the knot in step 4.

7 Repeat the pattern from steps 4–6 about 12 more times.

Repeat the First Pattern and Finish

8 Take the longer color A cord as the knotting cord, and continue tying a chain of

Adding a new knotting cord on an alternating DHHk chain

When you work on a chain of alternating DHHk or another similar chain, you'll use up the knotting cord very fast (for every 1"/2.5cm of chain, you'll use about 10"/25cm of cord). So when the knotting cord is about 12" (30cm) long and you still need more than 1" of the knotted chain, you may need to add a new one.

1 Leaving a 1" (2.5cm) tail, place the new knotting cord beside the holding cord **(a)**. Continue tying the alternating DHHk chain over these two cords for about ¾" (2cm).

2 Carefully pull the newly added cord from the bottom so the tail disappears inside the chain **(b)**. If you have pulled this cord a bit too much, tie a few more alternating DHHk.

3 Switch the knotting cords by making a half-hitch with each of them: Using the old knotting cord, make a half-hitch in the corresponding direction **(c)**. Then place this cord along with the holding cord. Using the new knotting cord, tie a half-hitch in the same direction as you did with the old knotting cord **(d)**. You have switched knotting cords.

4 Continue making the alternating DHHk chain for about ¾" before releasing the old knotting cord.

5 Bring the end of the old knotting cord toward the back of the chain, and trim it as close to the work as possible. You may have a short, visible end. To hide it, move the knots onto the chain and tuck this end inside the chain.

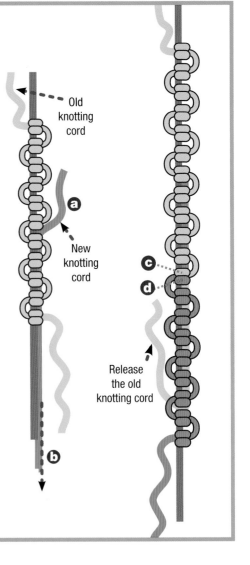

Old knotting cord

New knotting cord

Release the old knotting cord

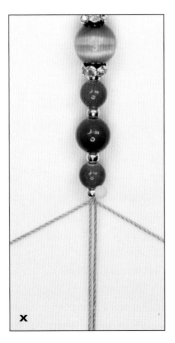

x

y

alternating DHHk until you have completed the second lap of the bracelet. Finish the bracelet the same way as the Zigzags and Spirals Bracelet.

Framing Beads with Square Knots Bracelet

1 Choosing whichever pattern you like, string and center the beads of your choice on two 15" (38cm) cords, creating a pattern 1" (2.5cm) shorter than the desired bracelet size.

2 Make a slip knot close to the beads on one end of

the cords. Pin the slip knot to the board.

3 Place and center one of the remaining cords under the other end of the beaded cords **[x]**. Tie a chain of only four or five square knots. Repeat on the other end of the cords.

4 To prevent the SQk chains from moving out of place, slide the chain and apply a drop of glue onto the holding cords right where they should rest **[y]**. Slide the knot back into place.

5 Finish the bracelet, braiding the cords' ends and making a sliding knot clasp as with the Zigzag Bracelet.

Rondelles and Twists Bracelet

1 Hold the 15" (38cm) cords together and string beads as desired [z].

2 Center the beads on the cords, and make a slip knot on one side close to the beads to keep them from moving. Pin the slip knot onto the board.

3 Place and center one of the remaining cords under the knotless ends to tie a series of four or five half knots. Slide down the chain into the holding cords, apply a dot of fabric glue,

and then slide the chain into place again [aa]. Keep knotting to create a spiral chain 1½" (4cm) long [bb].

When you are knotting a chain of half knots, the knots will turn toward one side, which creates the spiral. This makes it hard to tie normally. After six or seven half knots, I rotate the knotting cords and keep tying in the exact same way without changing the side on which the cord is folded.

4 Turn the piece to the other side, release the slip knot, and repeat step 3.

5 Finish the bracelet, braiding the cords' ends and making a sliding knot clasp in the same way as the Zigzag Bracelet.

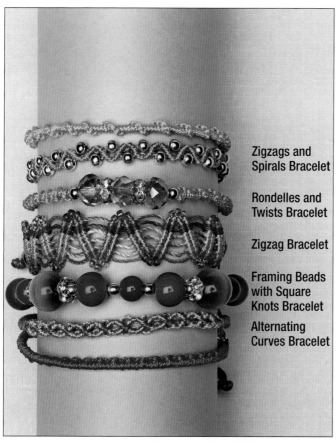

Zigzags and Spirals Bracelet

Rondelles and Twists Bracelet

Zigzag Bracelet

Framing Beads with Square Knots Bracelet

Alternating Curves Bracelet

z

aa

bb

Double Rainbow of Color
Necklace

Here's another great way to put basic and simple macramé knots to use! This project may help you remember what you learned before. The result will be this gorgeous and colorful double-strand necklace that is very easy to make.

MATERIALS & TOOLS
- **2** 20mm Swarovski crystal cosmic rings
- **2** end beads
- **4** 2" (5cm) headpins
- superglue
- fabric glue
- fray check
- embroidery needle
- flatnose pliers
- roundnose pliers
- flush cutters
- bent chainnose pliers
- marker pen
- scissors
- macramé board and pins

Short Necklace
- 0.5mm nylon cords
  - **2** 70" (1.78m) (filler cords)
  - **2** 130" (3.30m) (knotting cords)
- **4** 6mm round glass beads
- **2** 8mm round glass beads

Long Necklace
- 0.5mm nylon cords (strand A)
  - 50" (1.27m) (filler cord)
  - 105" (2.67m) (knotting cord)
- 0.5mm nylon cords (strand B)
  - 80" (2.03m) (filler cord)
  - 120" (3.05m) (knotting cord)
- **2** 8mm round glass beads (red)
- 8mm round glass bead (green)
- 8x10mm oval flat bead
- **2** 9x7.25mm ethnic barrel antique copper beads
- **2** 25x20mm oval faceted window glass beads
- 11x9mm round tube glass bead
- **2** 11mm round faceted glass beads
- **2** 35mm flat pendants
- **2** 11mm copper beads
- **2** 14x10mm faceted rondelle glass beads
- **2** 14mm round beads
- **2** 11x8mm faceted rondelle glass beads
- 8mm round stone bead

Material notes
Use nylon cord such as C-Lon beading cord, or S-Lon cord #18. The holes in the smaller beads (under 12mm) should fit at least three cords.

Short Necklace

The knotted/beaded strands of this necklace are created from the center outward. Each bead and knotted ring is separated by two square knots (SQk).

1 Fold a 70" (1.78m) cord in half, and attach it to a crystal ring with a loose lark's head knot (LHk) so the ring moves freely.

2 Place the 130" (3.30m) cord between the LHk so one end measures 30" (76cm). Take the ends of the newly added cord as the knotting cords to create two square knots (SQk) over the center cords (the filler cords) **[a]**.

3 Add a 6mm glass bead to the filler cords. Using the knotting cords, tie two SQk under the bead **[b]**.

Make a Knotted Ring

4 Using a marker, mark the ends of the filler cords. Because the cords' functions change throughout this section, I will refer to marked cords and unmarked cords.

The cords may be mixed up when you string them through the beads. It's important to mark and use the designated cords to avoid running out of one or more cords. If you need to add more cord, the best place to do it is between the beads. Tie the new cord with the one you need to replace, and hide the knot in the hole of the bead. Calculate about 10" (25cm) of cord for every 1" (2.5cm) of spiraled half-hitch chain.

5 Cross the two unmarked cords, use them as holding cords, and create two double half-hitch knots (DHHk) over them (use the marked cords as the knotting cords **[c, d]**) (Basics, p. 16). Release the slip knot, and gently pull the crossed cords until the loop disappears **[e]**.

6 Move the marked cords to the sides under the other cords **[f]**. From there, use them as the knotting cords to tie a chain of 10 vertical LHk on each side **[g]**. The knots on the chains should be facing outward.

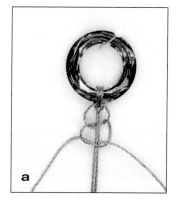

a

b

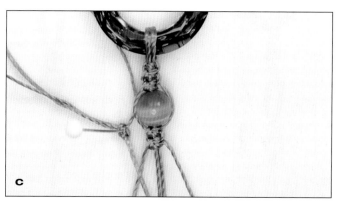

c

d

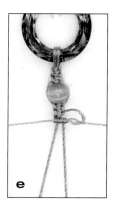

e

f

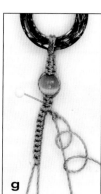

g

20 Place the 120" (3.05m) cord between the LHk so one of its ends measures 40" (1m) **[FIG 2]**. Secure the newly added cord by creating a half-hitch over the center cords with each end. The left cord makes a left-sided half-hitch, and the right cord makes a right-sided half-hitch **[s, t]**. Tighten.

Knotted Chain

21 Number the cords from 1–4 (from left to right). Use cord 2 as the holding cord and cord 1 as the knotting cord to tie two alternating DHHk, starting with a right-sided DHHk and then a left-sided DHHk **[u, v, FIG 3]**. End your knotting cords toward the left.

22 Repeat step 21 on the right side, in the opposite direction. Use cord 3 as the holding cord and cord 4 as the knotting cord to make two alternating DHHk, starting with a left-sided and then a right-sided DHHk **[w, x]**. End with the knotting cord toward the right.

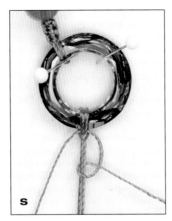

s

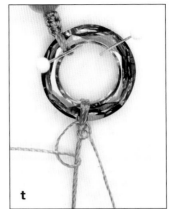

t

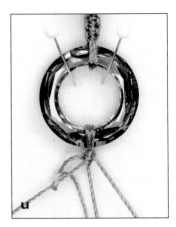

u

v

w

x

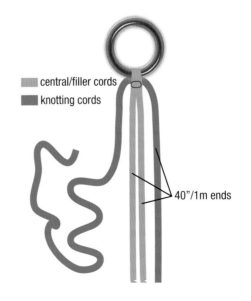

central/filler cords
knotting cords

40"/1m ends

FIG 2

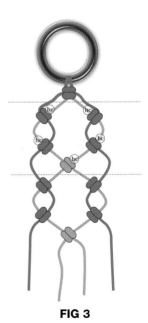

FIG 3

23 Finish and join the first motif, using the holding cords in the middle to create a DHHk. Tie the knot in the same direction every time you knot the central cords **[y, z]**.

24 Repeat steps 21–23 until this knotted chain, combined with the fifth bead for this sequence, measures the same length as the sequence of five beads on Strand A **[aa]**. Later on, dangling beads will be added to this piece of chain. Add the fifth bead directly after the knotted chain, and then tie two SQk below it **[bb]**.

25 Create a knotted ring as you did in steps 4–7 for the Short Necklace. Make a sequence of two beads and another knotted ring, and finish with the sequence of three beads in the pattern. Remember to tie two SQk

under each strung bead and knotted ring, placing the filler cords (marked cords) in the middle.

26 Shape the knotted rings as in step 13. Let dry.

27 String the last bead, and use the longest cord as the knotting cord to tie a spiraled chain of right- (or left) sided half-hitches until you have a length equal to Strand A.

Assemble the Necklaces

28 Lay the Long Necklace out, and lay the Short Necklace in the center of it, making sure the crystal rings and other components are facing to the right side.

29 Join the the loose ends on both short and long necklaces together with a DHHk, and then make 4" (10cm) braid (or longer if you want) on one side **[cc]**. Repeat with the loose ends on the other side.

30 Finish the braids and make a sliding knot clasp (Basics, p. 18) **[dd]**.

31 Complete the necklace by adding dangling beads to the knotted chain in Strand B. Space them evenly; I left three motifs before and after each dangling bead.

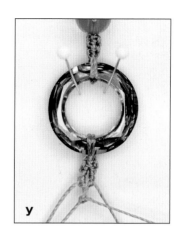

y

z

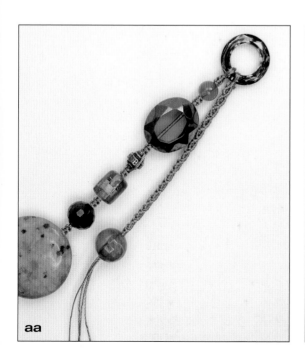

aa

bb

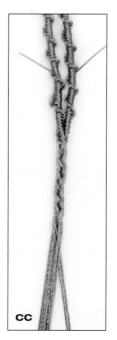

cc

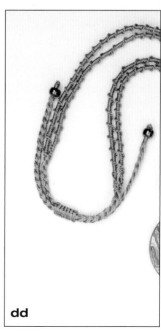

dd

Curvy Mother-of-Pearl
Bracelet

This curved form is the result of mixing glass pearls and a spacer bead with clear crystal accents. This combination and the micro macramé that holds it together all complete the overall dainty look of the bracelet.

MATERIALS & TOOLS

- **6** 40" (1m) 0.5mm nylon cords
- **14** 8mm large-hole glass pearls
- 14x12mm oval pearl box clasp
- **5** 6mm rondelle spacer beads
- **4** 11° seed beads
- fabric glue
- embroidery needle
- scissors
- macramé board and pins

Material note
Use C-Lon beading cord in one color.

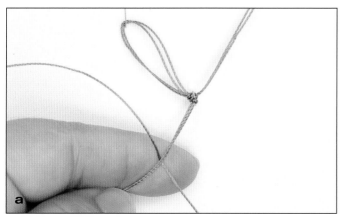

a

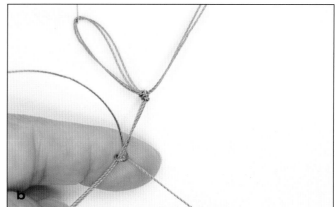

b

1 Use two of the 40" threads as holding cords, and tie a slip knot with them. Use a pin to secure these cords to the board through the knot.

2 Set the middle of another cord behind the holding cords **[a]**. Keep the cord in place by holding it between your index finger and thumb while you create the double half-hitch knot (DHHk) with your other hand **[b]**. Tighten and slide the cord close to the slip knot.

3 Attach the remaining cords in the same way: Add another cord, a pearl, a spacer bead, a pearl, and then the remaining two cords **[c]**. This is the central part of the bracelet.

4 Release the slip knot. Slide and center the mounted cords and the beads on the holding cords.

5 Pin the work so the beads are in a horizontal position, and make four equal groups of cords, placing one end of the holding cords in each group.

6 String a seed bead on the innermost strand in each of the two lower groups **[d]**.

7 With the left lower group, use the outermost cord as the holding cord to make a line of two DHHk toward the center. Make four more rows in the same manner for a total of five rows of DHHk. (In the following sections, you will tie six rows after the beads.)

8 Repeat with the right lower group **[e]**. (Use the outermost cord as the holding cord.)

9 String each of two central cords through a pearl in opposite directions, crossing the cords inside the bead **[f]**.

10 As in step 7, tie six diagonal rows of DHHk **[g]** on each side. Make sure the cords that pass through the bead are well-fastened without leaving any loops.

11 Bring each cord through from opposite ends, string a pearl, a spacer, and a pearl on the middle cords.

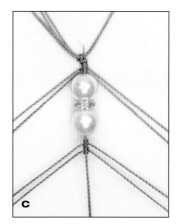

c

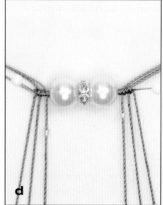

d

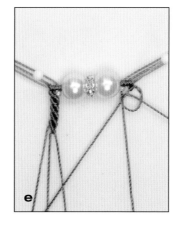

e

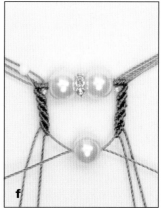

f

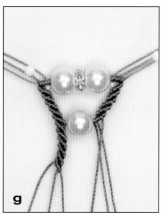

g

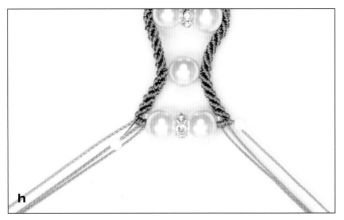

h

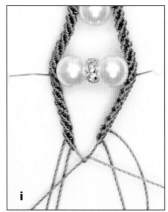

i

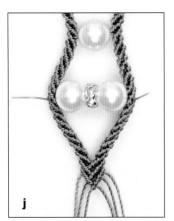

j

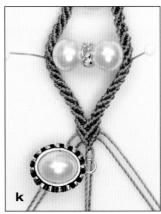

k

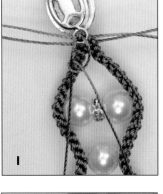

l

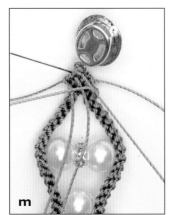

m

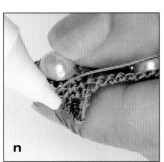

n

12 Knot six diagonal rows of DHHk on each side.

13 Repeat steps 9–11 **[h]**. After the last strung beads, tie eight rows of DHHk on each side.

14 Number the cords from 1–6 (left to right). Using cord 3 as the knotting cord and cord 4 as the holding cord, make a DHHk to join the two groups of strands in the middle **[i]**.

16 Use cord 1 as the holding cord to make a row of two DHHk from left to right.

17 On the opposite side, use cord 6 as the holding cord to create a row of three DHHk from right to left.

18 Repeat steps 16 and 17 one more time **[j]**. This completes one half of the bracelet.

19 Rotate the piece to work on the other half of the bracelet. Repeat steps 6–18.

20 Once you have finished both sides, measure the length of your bracelet and add the measurement of the clasp. If the piece is still short, tie more diagonal rows, distributing them evenly on each end, until you reach the desired length.

21 Add the clasp by stringing the central cords on the clasp's ring **[k]**. Turn the piece to the back, and using the central cords as the holding cords, tie two rows of DHHk **[l]**. Tie one to the right and one to the left **[m]**.

22 Secure the cords on the back of the piece. Thread them on an embroidery needle, and pass the cords through the knots on the back of the work. Pay special attention to the two center cords, making sure that they are well secured. Apply a coat of fabric glue **[n]**, let the glue dry, and cut off the excess cords.

projects
moving on

Petals in Autumn
Bracelet

In this beautiful autumn-inspired bracelet, the array of fall colors used to create the petals make them seem as if they are floating. Learn how to "hide" the working cords around the petals. Tiny seed beads give the petals a shiny look, and the bronze clasp complements the rest of the bracelet perfectly.

MATERIALS & TOOLS
- **9** 60" (1.52m) 0.5mm nylon cords
- 1g 11° seed beads in each of **5** colors
- **2** 12.5mm long end caps with ring
- extension chain for a bracelet
- **2** 4mm jump rings
- lobster claw clasp
- E6000 adhesive or Aleene's Jewelry & Metal Glue
- embroidery needle
- **2** pairs of flatnose pliers
- wire cutters
- scissors
- macramé board and pins

Materials note
Use nylon cord, such as C-Lon beading cord.
The end caps will fit 5–6mm cord.

Attach the End Cap

Note: If you use E6000 adhesive, start at least 24 hours prior to continuing with the rest of the project to let the glue fully cure. If you prefer an instant bond, use Aleene's Jewelry & Metal Glue. It bonds in seconds, so be prepared to join the knot to the end cap in the right position, quickly.

Read the manufacturer's directions before using glue. Apply glue in a well-ventilated area, avoiding contact with the skin. Clean the tip of the bottle or tube well so the lid does not get messy. While waiting for the glue to dry, it is also a good time to coat the tips of the cords with fray check.

1 Using all nine cords, make an overhand knot in the middle (30"/76cm). Adjust the knot by pulling each of the cords tight so the knot will fit into the end cap **[a]**.

2 Glue one end cap onto the knot. Let it dry **[b]**.

Start Knotting

3 Divide the strands into two equal sections. Start knotting outward on any section.

4 Make a double half-hitch knot (DHHk) with one cord over the rest of the cords to form a bundle **[c]**. Release that cord. Repeat, taking another cord from the bundle **[d]**, until you have only one cord left **[e]**. Repeat on the other section.

To tie each DHHk, choose a cord on the bottom of the bundle. It will wrap the bundle better.

Create the Petals

On each row of petals, both the petals and the DHHk alternate to the right or to the left. As you form the petals, cross the threads that hang down from one row to the next so they are not as visible **[f]**.

Cross the strands in pairs. Make an imaginary horizontal line over the pair of cords to be crossed to determine the length of their visibility. The cord that is more visible always goes below the one that is less visible.

Make the First Petal

5 Pin the work to the board and number the cords from 1–18. You will only use the six central cords to work on the first petal (cords 7–12). (Tie the DHHk from right to left.)

6 Using cord 12 as the holding cord, make a row of DHHk with cords: 10 (crossing it under cord 11), 11, 8 (crossing it over cord 9), 9, and 7 **[g]**.

7 Re-number the cords. Add 11º seed beads in the color of your choice: cord 8 (one), cord 9 (two), and cord 10 (one). This 11º pattern repeats throughout all petals.

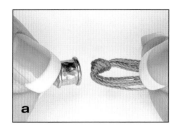

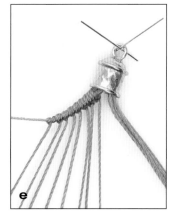
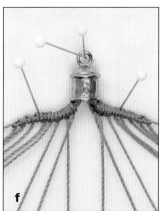
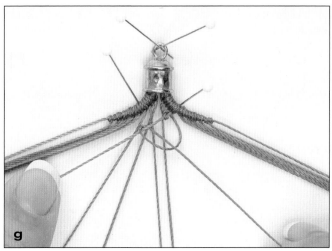

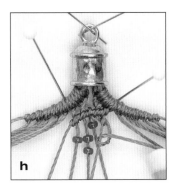

h

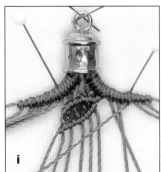

i

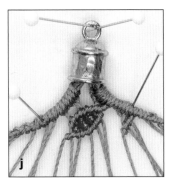

j

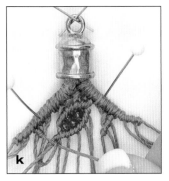

k

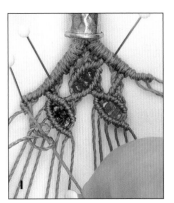

l

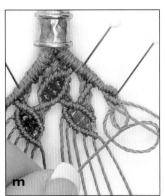

m

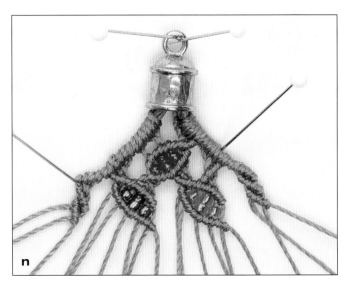

n

8 Enclose the 11º's with a row of DHHk, using cord 12 as the holding cord and cords 11–7 as the knotting cords **[h]**.

9 Using cord 15 as the holding cord, tie a small row of DHHk from right to left with cord 13 (crossing it under cord 14) and then with cord 14 **[i, j]**.

Make Two-Petal Rows

You will only use the 12 central cords to work on the petals (cords 4–15); the remaining three cords on each side are the floating cords. (The DHHk are tied from left to right.)

10 Re-number the cords from 1–18. Using cord 4 as the holding cord, make a row of DHHk with the following cords: 6 (crossing it under cord 5), 5, 7 **[k]**, 9 (crossing it under cord 8), and 8.

> When knotting with cord 7, be sure that the DHHk is as close to the tip of the petal in the previous row as possible to prevent any gaps or spaces. Keep this in mind while working on the rest of the petals in the bracelet.

11 Using cord 10 as the holding cord, tie a row of DHHk with the following cords: 12 (crossing it under cord 11), 11, 13, 15 (crossing it under cord 14), and 14.

12 Re-number the cords, and string 11º's on cords 6, 7, and 8, and also on cords 12, 13, and 14, following the pattern as in the first petal.

13 Enclose the beads with a row of DHHk, starting with cord 4 as the holding cord and using cords 5, 6, 7, 8, and 9 as the knotting cords. Repeat, using cord 10 as the holding cord, to make a row of DHHk with the following cords: 11, 12, 13, 14, and 15.

Floating Cords

Both sections are knotted diagonally from left to right.

14 Place a pin by cord 1 to prevent the corner from folding. Using cord 1 as the holding cord, make a small diagonal row of DDHk, with cord 3 (crossing it under cord 2) and then with cord 2 **[l]**. Tie a second row below the previous one in the same way, but without crossing the cords.

15 Tie another short row of DDHk, using cord 16 as the holding cord and cords 17 and 18 as the knotting cords. Make a second row below the previous one **[m, n]**. On the next rows of two petals, cross cord 18 under cord 17 before making the DHHk, and then continue as before.

Make Three-Petal Rows

(The DHHk are tied from right to left.)

16 Re-number the cords from 1–18.
Petal 1: Using cord 6 as the holding cord, make a line of

DHHk with the following cords: 4 (crossing it under cord 5), 5, 3, 1 (crossing it under cord 2), and 2 **[o]**.

Petal 2: Using cord 12 as the holding cord, make a line of DHHk with the following cords: 10 (crossing it under cord 11), 11, 9, 7 (crossing it under cord 8), and 8 **[p]**.

Petal 3: Using cord 18 as the holding cord, make a line of DHHk with the following cords: 16 (crossing it under cord 17), 17, 15, 13 (crossing it under cord 14), and 14.

17 Re-number the cords, and add seed beads to cords 2, 3, and 4; cords 8, 9, and 10; and cords 14, 15, and 16, as in the previous petals.

18 Surround the beads with a diagonal row of DHHk, starting with cord 6 as the holding cord and cords 5, 4, 3, 2, and 1 as the knotting cords **[q]**.

Repeat, using cord 12 as the holding cord, to knot a row of DHHk with cords 11, 10, 9, 8, and 7.

Repeat again, this time using cord 18 as the holding cord and cords 17, 16, 15, 14, and 13 as the knotting cords **[r]**.

19 Determine the length of the knotted work: First, subtract the length of the clasp and twice the length of the first petal (assume that the length of the last petal will be the same as the length of the first one). Be sure to include the

length of the split rings, jump rings, and both cord ends in the clasp measurement. For example, if you want to create a 6" (15cm) bracelet, and your end petals and clasp measurement is 2" (5cm), the length of the knotted work should be 4" (7.6cm). (Measure the knotted rows of petals from the bottom of the first petal to the bottom of a two-petal row.) Knot the last petal when you need about an inch or less to finish. If you need more than an inch, repeat the pattern once or as many times as necessary.

20 Repeat the pattern, alternating two-petal and three-petal rows, until complete. Remember to make the variation in step 17. For the last petal, even the right-hand side of the last row of two petals by making two diagonal lines of DHHk. Use cords 16–18; using cord 16 as the holding cord, tie a small row of DHHk from left to right with cord 18 crossing it under cord 17, and then with cord 17. Next, using the same holding cord, make a second row in the opposite direction using the two cords to the left. Cross the cords as you did before.

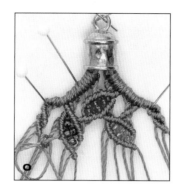
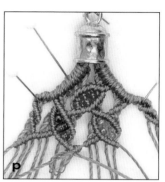

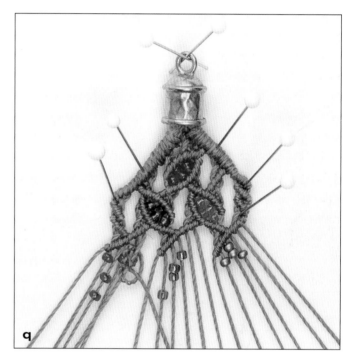

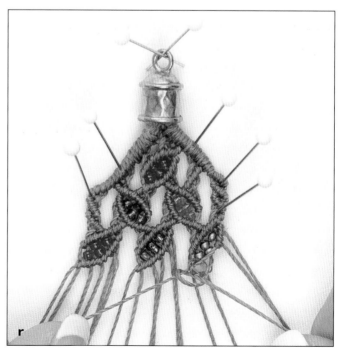

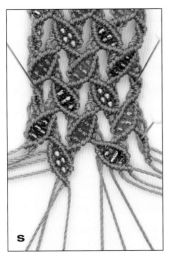

s

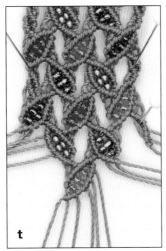

t

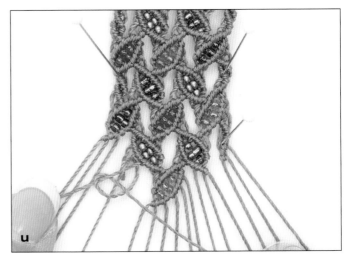

u

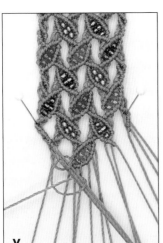

v

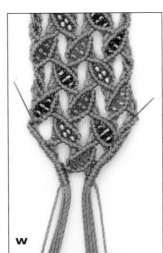

w

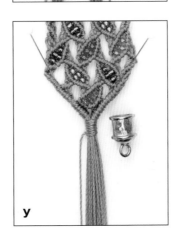

x

y

Make the Last Petal

Knot the last petal with the six central cords (cords 7–12). The DHHk are tied from right to left **[s]**.

21 Using cord 12 as the holding cord, tie a row of DHHk with the following cords: 10 (crossing it under cord 11), 11, 9, 7 (crossing it over cord 8), and 8.

22 Re-number the cords. Add 11ºs to cord 8 (one), cord 9 (two) and cord 1 (one).

23 Enclose the seed beads with a row of DHHk, using cord 12 as the holding cord and cords 11–7 as the knotting cords **[t]**.

24 Using cord 6 as the holding cord, tie a small row of DHHk from right to left with cord 4 (crossing it under cord 5) and then with cord 5 **[u]**.

Finish

25 Re-number all the cords from 1–18, and divide them into two equal sections. Using cord 1 as the holding cord, tie a diagonal row of accumulating knots (Basics, p. 14) from left to right until cord 9 is knotted. With the accumulating knots, the cords should be crossed as in previous steps **[v]**. Repeat on the right side, starting with cord 18 as the holding cord in an inward direction and ending in the middle **[w]**.

26 Choose one of the last knotting cords to make an alternating DHHk chain over the rest of the cords, forming a bundle **[x]**. Adjust the chain to fit the end cap **[y]**.

27 Secure the last knotting cord by threading it on an embroidery needle and passing the needle through the back part of a few cords in the chain. Work from the top down so the needle and the cord come out in the same direction as the rest of the cords **[z]**.

28 Glue the end cap, folding the cords to the back **[aa]**. When it is dry, cut the excess cords as close as possible to the cap **[bb]**.

29 Use two pairs of pliers to open a jump ring. Insert the end cap and the extender chain into the open ring. Close the ring **[cc]**.

30 Attach a lobster claw clasp to the other end of the bracelet with a jump ring **[dd]**.

z

aa

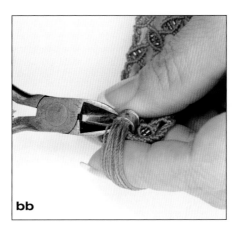

bb

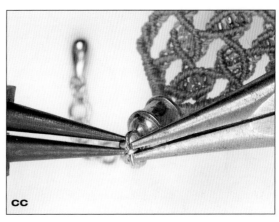

cc

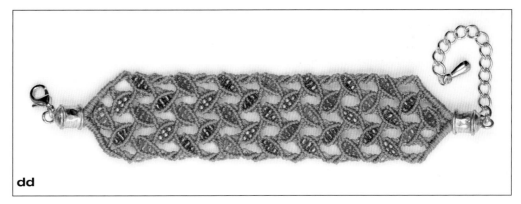

dd

Whimsical Wheels *Earrings*

A capricious combination of colors makes these earrings stand out. They are versatile and light-weight, and will look great in lots of different colors. Swarovski crystals add sparkle to the wheels, so this unique design is sure to make a statement.

MATERIALS & TOOLS
- **10** 40" (1m) 0.5mm nylon cords
- **30** 3mm Swarovski bicone crystals
- beads to add to the earring wires (optional)
- pair of 15x38mm kidney earring wires
- embroidery needle
- fabric glue or superglue
- flatnose pliers
- scissors
- macramé board and pins

Materials notes
Use nylon cord, such as C-Lon beading cord, in four or five different colors. Divide the cords, using five for each earring.

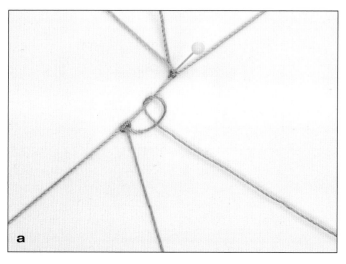

a

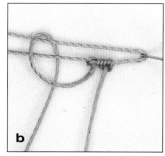

b

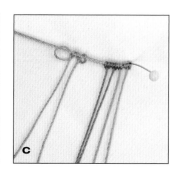

c

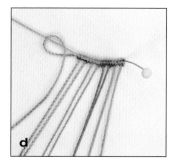

d

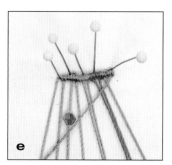

e

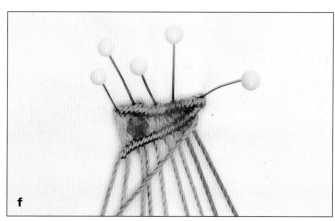

f

Mount the Cords

1 Make a slip knot in the center of one of the cords, using it as the holding cord to attach the remaining cords, and pin the knot onto the board.

2 Attach one of the remaining cords with a reverse lark's head knot (LHk). Take the right end of this cord to make a half-hitch on the holding cord **[a]**. Release the slip knot, and place a pin in the middle of the holding cord. Bringing that end to the left hand side, make a half-hitch with the left end of the mounted cord to complete the mounting knot **[b]**. The two ends of the holding cord are to the left.

3 Attach the remaining cords over the two ends of the holding cord. Fold the cords in half, and add them with a reverse LHk with half-hitch **[c]**.

4 After you have attached all the cords, use one of the holding cords to make a DHHk over the other one **[d]**.

5 Pin the work to the board in a horizontal position. Starting from the left, string a 3mm crystal on the third cord **[e]**.

6 Using the rightmost cord as the holding cord for each row, create two rows of DHHk below the crystal **[f]**. As you knot, the piece will take on a curved shape. Reposition the work as needed while you knot.

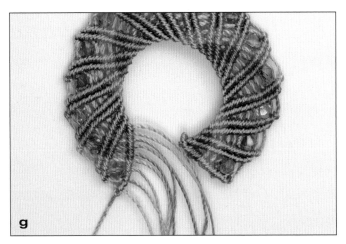

g

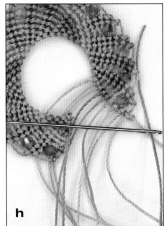

h

i

7 Repeat steps 5 and 6 13 more times. Then, add a crystal as in step 5. Make only one row of DHHk to enclose the crystal **[g]**.

Finish

8 Turn the piece over. One at a time, thread a cord on an embroidery needle. Pass through the back part of the mounted cords to close the circle. Start with the cords in the middle of the row, matching the color cord with the back knot on the piece, and continue with the remaining cords **[h, i]**. Pull the cords gently so both ends of the wheel join together **[j]**.

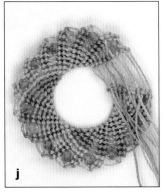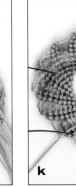

j

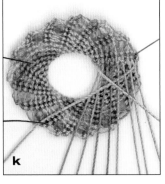

k

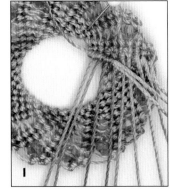

l

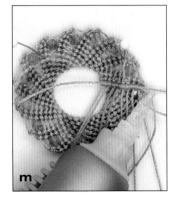

m

n

o

9 Cross the outermost cords. Using them as the holding cords, tie a horizontal line of DHHk over both cords, using the rest of the threads. Don't adjust the knots too much. Cross two cords to make DHHk over them (Basics, p. 16) **[k, l]**.

10 Before pulling the loop through completely,

apply a dot of superglue (let the drop sit) **[m]**, or a generous amount of fabric glue on the portion of the cord that will go inside the DHHk row; pull the cord until the loop is gone. Let it dry and clip the holding cords close to the sides. For extra security, before trimming off these leftover cords, secure their ends under the last row of DHHk **[n]**.

11 Apply glue to the back side of the last DHHk row. When the glue has dried, cut the excess cords.

12 Attach the earring wires to the wheels, and press the loop on the wires where the wheel rests so it does not come out. If desired, add some beads to the earring wires **[o]**.

Window Glass
Necklace

This project is a perfect example of less is more. You will learn how to make a micro-macramé bezel around a large glass bead (or any stone you like) using square knots and vertical lark's head knots.

MATERIALS & TOOLS

- 0.5mm nylon cords
  - **4** 35" (89cm) color A
  - **3** 35" color B
  - 20" (51cm) color B
  - 10' (3.05m) color A or B
- 20" (51cm) 2mm cord
- 25x30mm faceted window glass bead
- extension chain for necklace
- **2** 4mm jump rings
- **2** 4mm inside diameter fold-over crimp with loop
- lobster claw clasp
- superglue
- fabric glue
- scissors
- macramé board and pins

Material notes

Use nylon cord such as C-Lon beading cord or #5 Tuff cord in two different colors. Choose a large bead like I have, or replace with a stone or other component of your choice.

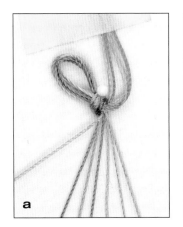

a

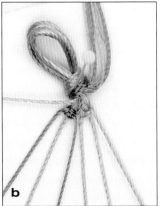

b

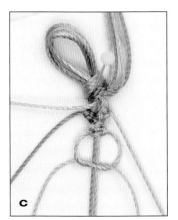

c

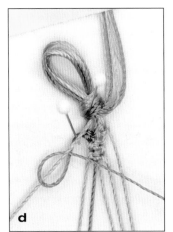

d

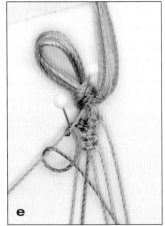

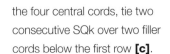

e

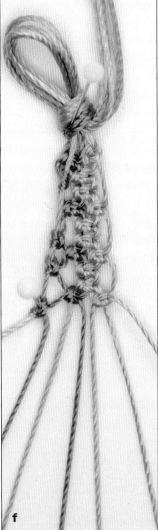

f

FIG 1

Knotted Bezel

1 Make a slip knot with all of the 35" (89cm) 0.5mm cords together, leaving a 12" (30cm) tail. Pin the knot onto the board, and tape the tail ends on top of it.

2 Choose a color A cord to be the wrapping cord, and set it aside to the left. Arrange the rest of the cords, alternating the color B and color A cords **[a]**.

3 Make a row of two square knots (SQk) using three cords per knot **[b]**.

4 Ignore the two outer cords (floating cords), and using the four central cords, tie two consecutive SQk over two filler cords below the first row **[c]**.

5 Using the left floating cord, make a right-sided vertical lark's head knot (LHk) **[FIG 1]** over the wrapping cord (the cord set aside in step 2) **[d, e]**. Set this cord aside again. Place a pin where you want this knot, and adjust it against the pin.

6 Repeat steps 3–5 **[f]** until the knotted piece wraps around the bead at its widest part **[g]**. Finish the piece with a row of two SQk using three cords per knot as in step 3. Release the slip knot.

g

7 Add the 20" (51cm) wrapping cord on the right side of the piece. Thread the cord on an embroidery needle, and pass it through the spaces left by the floating cords from the back to the front repeatedly until this cord reaches the other end of the piece **[h, i]**. Center the cord on the knotted piece.

8 Make overhand knots on the four ends of the wrapping cords to identify them later when all the cords are bundled.

9 Center and secure the two ends of the wrapping cord on the front with a SQk **[j]**. Repeat with the two ends of the wrapping cords on the back **[k]**.

10 Use the two ends of the wrapping cords as the filler cords and one cord from each side of the edge in the knotted piece to make a SQk. Repeat on the back.

Necklace Rope

You can change the rope measurements as desired. The 10' (3.05m) cord used as the knotting cord is long enough to add a few inches to each side of the rope **[l]**.

11 Hold all of the cords together. Attach the 12 ft. (3.05m) cord by its center to this bundle using a DHHk.

12 Separate the bundled cords into two equal

h

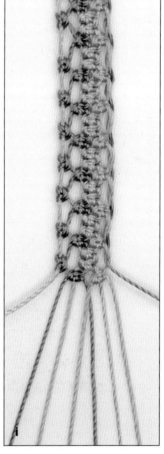

i

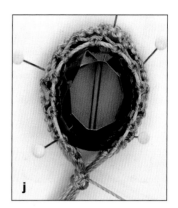

j

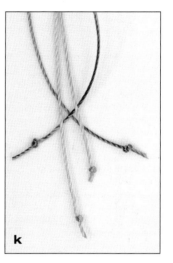

k

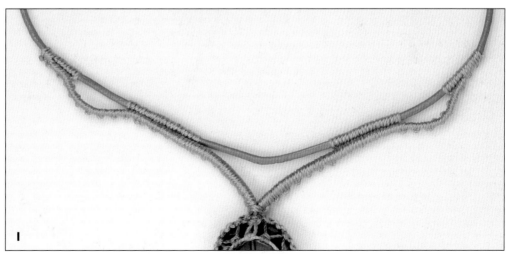

l

groups. If necessary, adjust the filler cords from the last SQk (step 10); these are the ends of the wrapping cords with the overhand knots on the tips.

13 Work on the left group of cords: Use the newly

added cord end as the knotting cord to make an alternating DHHk chain over the bundled cords **[m]**. Repeat until the chain measures about 1" (2.5cm) and the end of the knotting cord is toward the right.

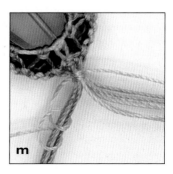

m

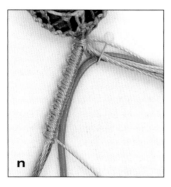

n

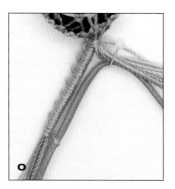

o

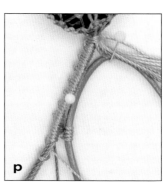

p

is shorter than the alternating DHHk chain so it forms a curve **[q]**.

18 Join both the 2mm cord and the bundled cords as one, and then tie three alternating DHHk over the cords **[r]**.

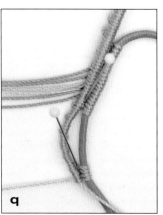

q

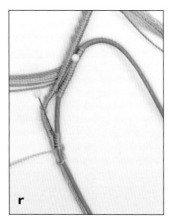

r

14 Place the 2mm cord in the middle of the pendant and leaving about ¾" (1.9cm) or less from its center, take the knotting cord to tie a right-sided DHHk over this cord, next to the last DHHk tied to the bundled cords **[n, o]**.

15 Change the knotting cord to the left and make a row of vertical DHHk over the 2mm cord, using the bundled cords as the holding cords. Continue alternating the direction of the rows **[p]**. As you knot this segment, release the cords, two at a time, from the bundle until you only have two left. Make sure the released cords are pointing toward the center of this segment (which should measure ¾").

16 With the knotting cord in the middle of the 2mm cord and bundled cords, continue making alternating DHHk over the two holding cords left from the bundle only (for about ¾").

17 Join the 2mm cord again and make about three rows of vertical DHHk over this cord and the bundled cords. The distance of the 2mm cord

19 Thread the end of the knotting cord through an embroidery needle, and pass it through the knots on the back of the chain **[s]**. As you pull the knotting cord, a loop will form. When this loop measures about ½" (13mm), apply superglue to the part of the cord that will go through the knots; let the small drop of glue sit while you pull the cords through. Repeat with the right group of cords.

Finish

20 Apply fabric glue to the released cords in step 15. Let it dry, and trim the excess cords **[t]**.

21 Cover the ends of the 2mm cord with fold-over crimps, making sure that the folding sides are on the back.

22 Add a split ring and an extension chain to one end, and a split ring and a lobster clasp on the other end (Basics, p. 19) **[u]**.

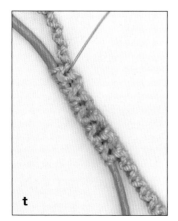

s

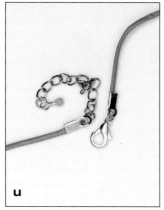

t

u

Antiqued Copper Caviar
Bracelet

the
orde

9

leng

10

corc
kno
step
cent

11

from
From
the
six [

12

side
corc
that

Fir

13

two
loop
clas

14

One
on a
pass
back
patt
each

15

emb
throu

The beauty, elegance, and simplicity of this bracelet comes from the combination of metal seed beads with thread. Choose a hook-and-eye clasp in the same shade of copper to complete the look. The project is fairly simple to complete, since it is mostly made up of square knots—the challenge is to combine materials and colors, harmoniously.

MATERIALS & TOOLS
- 0.5mm nylon cords
  - **4** 45" (1.14m)
  - **2** 60" (1.52m)
- 10g 8° metal seed beads
- 29mm hook-and-eye clasp
- superglue
- Aleene's Fabric Fusion glue
- fray check
- scissors
- macramé board and pins

Material notes
Use nylon cord such as C-Lon beading cord, or S-Lon cord #18. Four cords will function only as filler cords, so they will remain inactive through the work.

Splendor in the Loom
Bracelet

This distinctive loom-style bracelet is curious and intricate with different colored metal and glass seed beads. This knotting method allows you to create your own patterns, and the color choices offer endless possibilities.

MATERIALS & TOOLS

- 0.5mm nylon cords
  4 30" (76cm)
  10' (3.05m)
- 30mm slide clasp (22mm length of bar)
- 8º seed beads
  20g color A (black metal)
  3g color B (red)
  7g color C (green)
- superglue
- fabric glue
- fray check
- permanent marker

- tweezers
- embroidery needle
- wire cutters
- scissors
- masking tape (optional)
- macramé board and pins

Material notes

Use nylon cord such as C-Lon beading cord, or S-Lon cord #18. You should be able to pass the cords through the 8º seed bead holes more than once. If you choose your own pattern, calculate the amount of the beads accordingly. There are approximately 19 metal seed beads per gram and 35 glass seed beads per gram.

Attach the Cords

First, coat the tips of all the cords with fray check to make it easier to string the beads.

1 Fold three 30" (76cm) cords in half. Tie them onto the clasp's bar with reverse lark's head knots (LHks), then make a triple half-hitch knot (THHk) with each end **[a]**. This will fill the bar with the mounted cords and provide separation to the strands so the beads fit without piling up on each other. The six ends are the holding cords.

2 Find the middle of the last 30" cord, backtrack 3" (7.5cm) to one end, and tie a slip knot. Pin this knot to the board, and use a piece of masking tape to keep the end of the cord out of the way. Using the longer end as the knotting cord, tie a vertical double half-hitch knot (DHHk) over the first holding cord **[b]**. String a color A 8º seed bead on the knotting cord. Repeat this vertical DHHk/A pattern **[c]** throughout the row. Apply superglue to the back side of the knots on the outermost parts of the clasp's bar to keep them from loosening and sliding toward the top part of the bar.

3 Release the slip knot and string an A on each end of this cord. Number these eight holding cords from 1–8 (from left to right) **[d]**.

4 Tie a slip knot 6" (15cm) from one end of the 10' (3.05m) cord. Pin and tape the knot to the board, close to cord 1. This is the runner cord. Use the longest end of this cord as the knotting cord to tie a row of vertical DHHk over the eight holding cords **[e]**. On this row, no beads will be added between the vertical DHHk, but leave some space as if there were beads there **[f]**.

Make the Beaded Pattern

Always keep the holding cords taut, and use the same tension consistently when knotting and adjusting the vertical DHHk.

5 Untie the slip knot from the left side of the runner cord, and string the seed beads, following the pattern on **FIG 1 (row 1)** on the holding cords. Insert the left short end of the runner cord into the first bead and the long end through the last bead of the row **[g]**.

6 Using the runner cord as the knotting cord, make a vertical DHHk over cord 8 toward the left **[h]**. Insert the seed beads onto the runner cord, following the pattern on

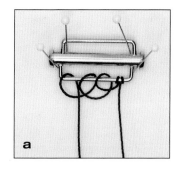
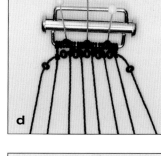

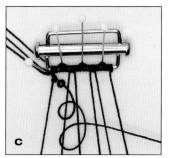

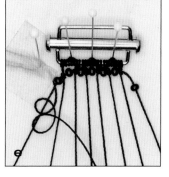
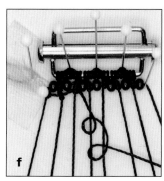

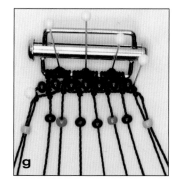

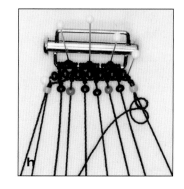

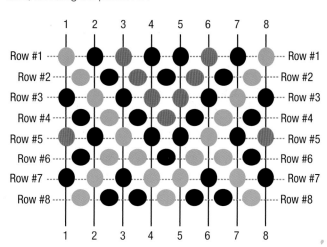

FIG 1

61

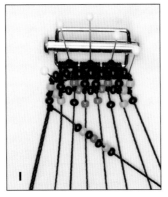

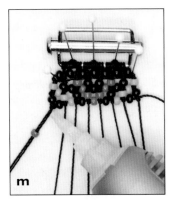

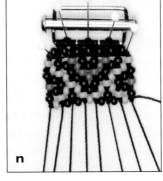

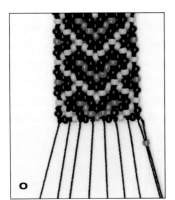

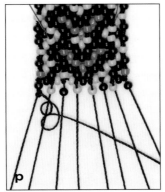

row 2. Leaving a distance of approximately 15" (38cm), tie a slip knot below the beads.

7 Slide the next 8º on the runner cord close to the knot on cord 8. Again, using the runner cord as the knotting cord, tie a vertical DHHk over cord 7 toward the left. Repeat **[i]** until you reach cord 1. Make the vertical DHHk over cord 1 and the short end of the runner cord together **[j]**. In the following rows, hold these two cords as one. As you finish this step, the runner cord is to the left.

> Because the runner cord is long and many beads are strung on it, you may want to use the passive knotting cord method (Basics, p. 16).

8 String the 8º s on the holding cords, following the pattern in row 3. String both the long and short ends of the runner cord through the first strung 8º **[k]**.

9 Using the long end of the runner cord as the knotting cord, make a vertical DHHk over cord 1 and the short end beside it. String the 8º s, following row 4 in the pattern, on the runner cord **[l]**. Repeat as in step 7, sliding an 8º from the runner cord and knotting vertical DHHk over the next holding cord to the right.

10 After several rows, before you string the next 8º on cord 1, apply a drop of glue (superglue or fabric glue) where the 8º should be sitting, and then slide the 8º in place **[m]**. Trim this short end.

11 Continue working the next rows, following and repeating the pattern **[n]**, until you have reached the desired length. At the end of each row, insert the runner cord onto the bead below before working on the next row **[o]**.

Narrow the Width

12 Following the pattern, string 8º s on the holding cords. Using the runner cord, make a row of vertical DHHk over the holding cords from left to right (don't string 8º s on the runner cord) **[p, q]**.

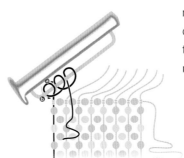

FIG 2

13 Make another vertical DHHk over cord 8 in the opposite direction **[r]**. Insert seven As onto the runner cord **[s]**, and make a slip knot, leaving a length of about 15" (38cm).

14 Slide an 8º, and tie a vertical DHHk over the next holding cord. Repeat this step until you have completed the row.

Finish

15 Turn the piece to the back, placing the holding cords toward the top. Put the other half of the clasp above the holding cords, with the bar facing down. Make sure the clasp is facing the right way.

16 Set the runner cord aside. From left to right, attach the holding cords to the bar's clasp with THHk **[FIG 2]**: Starting with the first holding cord, pass the end over and around the bar's clasp from front to back. Bring the end back toward the front, passing it to the left side of itself. Tighten the loop, making sure the clasp is positioned as close to the work as possible. That makes the first half-hitch. Using your thumb and index finger, grab the loop against the bar's clasp to keep it in place while you make two more half-hitches to complete the knot. Repeat with the remaining holding cords.

q

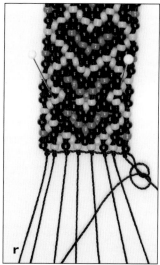

r

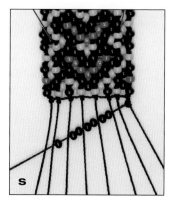

s

t

17 Still working on the back, secure the cords, one by one, including the runner cord: Thread the first cord onto an embroidery needle to pass it through a knot in the row below. Repeat with the rest of the cords. Apply a generous amount of fabric glue over the knots the cords have passed through and on the THHk made onto the bar's clasp **[t]**. Let the glue dry, and then cut off the excess cords.

Adding a new runner cord

Many times, despite careful calculations, the runner cord can be too short. Add a new runner cord as follows: Leave the old runner cord when you have completed a row. The new runner cord will be added to the opposite side. Taking the new cord, fold it so one end is approximately 10" (25cm). Mount the cord, using reverse LHk, with the short end to the bottom. Hold the short end with the holding cord next to it as if they were one. After a few rows, add the corresponding seed bead as in step 10, apply glue, and cut the short end. Do the same with the old runner cord. Continue working.

Shades of the Sea
Bracelet

In this charming bracelet, various shades of rich blue peek through the open-work knotting and the knots that frame each diamond-shaped glass bead. The sliding knot clasp completes the bracelet, which is both simple and easy to make. You will enjoy mixing and matching the cords and glass beads in this project as you learn a different way of joining motifs—bundling and releasing the cords in between each diamond shape.

MATERIALS & TOOLS
- 0.5mm nylon cords
  - **10** 35" (89cm), **2** each of **5** different colors
  - **2** 40" (1m) in the same color
- **3** 16x8mm diamond-shaped glass beads
- **2** 6mm cord end beads
- superglue
- fabric glue
- scissors
- macramé board and pins

Materials note
Use nylon cord as C-Lon beading cord, or S-Lon cord #18. Start and end with the 40" (1m) cords.

Make the Bracelet

1 Hold the cords together as one, find the middle, and tie a slip knot (two cords are longer than the rest). Pin the knot to the board and tape the loose ends on top.

2 Using one of the longer cords, make two alternating double half-hitch knots (DHHk) below the slip knot to form a bundle **[a]**.

3 Separate the cords (one of each color) into two equal sections.

4 Make two alternating DHHk on each section to form two bundles. On the left section, using the same color cord that you used to tie the bundle in step 2 as the knotting cord, make two alternating DHHk over the rest of the cords. Start with a left-sided DHHk followed by a right-sided DHHk; then release this cord. Repeat on the right section, taking the same color cord as in the left side and making two alternating DHHk over the rest of the cords. Start with a right-sided DHHk, followed by a left-sided DHHk; then release this cord **[b]**.

5 Release the remaining cords from the bundles on the left and right sides. Starting on either side, make a DHHk with one cord over the cords in the bundle; then release this cord **[c]**. Repeat with the remaining cords until there is one holding cord left. Repeat on

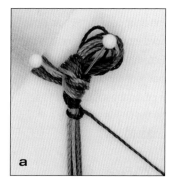

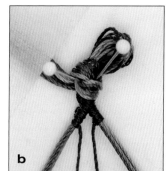

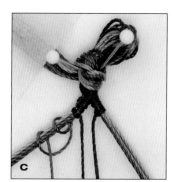

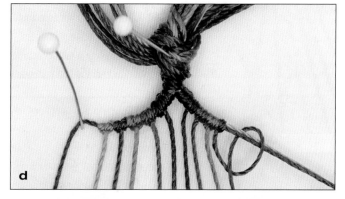

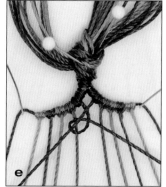

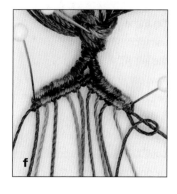

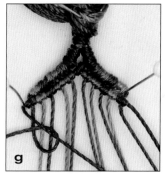

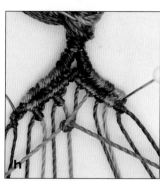

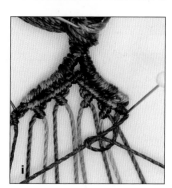

the other side. (You can release the cords in the same order on both the left and right sides **[d]**.) Choose the cord you want to release from the bundle, place, and arrange it under the rest of the cords on the bundle; then make the DHHk.

6 Number the cords from 1–12 (from left to right).

7 From the center to the left, using cord 7 as the holding cord, tie a row of six diagonal DHHk **[e]**.

8 Re-number the cords and repeat on the right side: Using cord 7 as the holding cord, make a line of five DHHk toward the right **[f]**.

9 Make six pairs out of the 12 cords.

10 On the left side, in each of the three pairs, the left cord is the holding cord (cords 1, 3, and 5). Place a pin to the right of cord 1 to create a sharp angle, and using cord 2 as the knotting cord, tie a DHHk **[g]**.

Make a DHHk on the other two pairs of cords.

11 Repeat on the right side. Make a DHHk on each of the three pairs. In each pair,

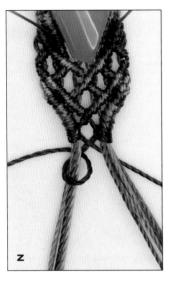

z

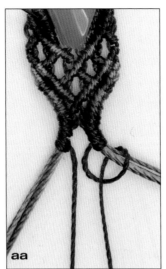

aa

bb

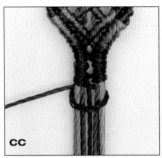

cc

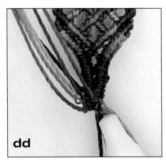

dd

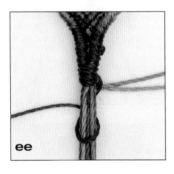

ee

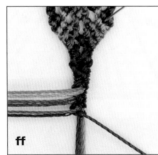

ff

gg

24 At the end of the last motif, take any of the last knotting cords to tie a DHHk over all the cords, making one bundle [cc]. Apply fabric glue to a small length (about 10mm) of the bundled cords [dd]. (Do not apply glue to the knotting cord.) Make sure the cords inside the bundle are well covered. Let the glue dry fully. Do the same on the other end of the bracelet.

25 On one end, using the same knotting cord, continue making one alternating DHHk, then release two cords from the back side of the bundle [ee]. Repeat until you have released six cords [ff].

26 Cut the released cords. Apply more fabric glue over these ends, if desired.

27 Repeat steps 25 and 26 on the other end of the bracelet.

28 Braid the six cords on each end [gg] to make a sliding knot clasp (Basics, p. 18).

22 Take the knotting cords from each side, cross them under the bundles, and tie two alternating DHHk over each bundle. Start with a DHHk facing outward [z], and then tie a DHHk facing the center [aa].

23 Now the cords are in position to make the next motif. Repeat steps 3–22 to make two more motifs [bb].

Sandy Beach in Paradise
Bracelet

This intricate design results in a fun and easy bracelet. The color pallet possibilities are enormous, and the knotting brings the colors together harmoniously. A variety of textures and styles combine and blend to complement each other. This is a delightful and interesting project once you are familiar with the pattern.

MATERIALS & TOOLS
- 0.5mm nylon cords
  55" (1.40m)
  12 35" (89cm) or **6** 64" (1.63m)
  (see material notes)
- **4 or 5** 8x6mm faceted crystal rondelles
- 24–30 4mm round beads
- **2** 8° metal seed beads
- 11° seed beads
  2g color A
  1g color B
- extension chain for a bracelet
- lobster-claw clasp

- **2** 6mm split rings
- **2** 4mm jump rings
- embroidery needle
- superglue
- fabric glue
- fray check
- scissors
- macramé board and pins

Material notes

Use nylon cord such as C-Lon beading cord, or S-Lon cord #18. If you want individual colors, use 35" (89cm) cords. If you want two of the same color cords next to each other, use 64" (1.63m) cords in that color.

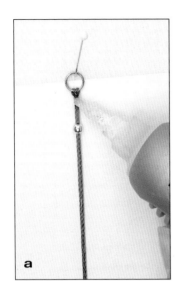

FIG 1

FIG 2

FIG 3

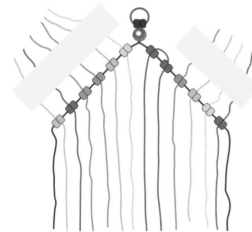

FIG 4

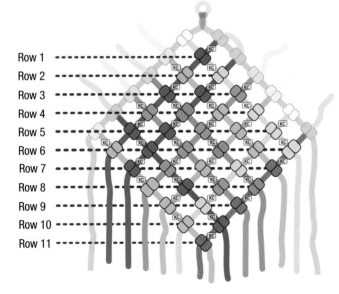

FIG 5 (KC = knotting cord)

Mount the Cords

1 Fold the 55" (1.40cm) in half, and attach it to one of the split rings with a lark's head knot (LHk). Both ends of this cord will be the mounting cords.

2 String an 8º metal seed bead on each cord end, apply a drop of superglue below the LHk, and then slide the 8º over the glue [a].

3 Attach the single cords in the desired order with DHHk or LHk [FIG 1, FIG 2], leaving a 3" (7.6cm) tail. If the cords are doubled, attach them using reverse LHk with half-hitch [FIG 3].

4 Tape the loose tails of the single cords out of the way on top of the piece [FIG 4]. Coat about 1¼" (3cm) of the working cords' tips with fray check.

Make the Diamond

On the following five rows, you will increase the amount of knots by adding one cord from each side. Pair the cords before knotting, and tie a DHHk with each pair. Make the knots in the same direction on each row—

then on the next row, in the opposite direction. This means that all the even rows are knotted one way and the odd rows are knotted the opposite way. After row 6, release one cord to each side to decrease the amount of knots in the rows [FIG 5].

5 Begin knotting.
Row 1: Find the two center cords and tie a DHHk, using the right cord as the knotting cord [b].
Row 2: Adding one cord from each side, separate the four cords into two pairs and tie two DHHk, using the left cords as the knotting cords [c].
Row 3: Make three pairs out of the six center cords to create three DHHk, using the right cords as the knotting cords [d].
Row 4: Pair the eight center cords and tie four DHHk, using the left cords as the knotting cords [e].
Row 5: Pair the 10 center cords and make five DHHk, using the right cords as the knotting cords [f].
Row 6: Pair the 12 center cords and tie six DHHk, using the left cords as the knotting cords [g].

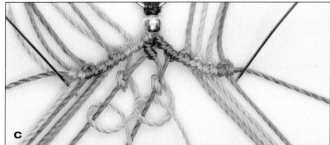

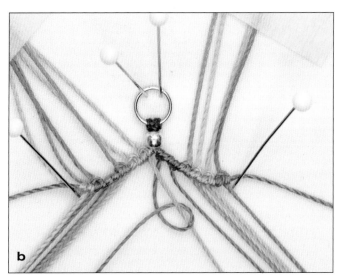

After the sixth row, decrease the amount of knots on every row by releasing one cord to each side (pair the cords on each row before knotting).

Row 7: Repeat row 5.
Row 8: Repeat row 4.
Row 9: Repeat row 3.
Row 10: Repeat row 2.
Row 11: Repeat row 1.

6 Finish this section with two diagonal lines of DHHk on each side. Use a pin to keep the diamond shape at the beginning of the rows. Start on the left side, using the leftmost cord as the holding cord. Tie a row of DHHk, using the six next cords as the knotting cords, from left to right **[h]**.

7 Repeat on the right side, using the outermost right cord as the holding cord. Make a diagonal row of DHHk toward the center, using the seven next cords as the knotting cords.

8 Repeat steps 6 and 7 to create a second line of DHHk on each side **[i]**.

Make the Beaded Section

This section has two knotted segments on the outer sides. You may want to enclose the beads after those segments are completed or right after you string the beads onto the central cords.

9 Number the cords from 1–14 and string the beads as follows: four color A 11º seed beads on cord 1 and cord 14, a 4mm bead on cords 2 and 3, a 4mm bead on cords 12 and 13, approx. 11 color B 11º seed beads on cord 4 and cord 11, approximately seven As on cord 6 and cord 9, and a 6x8mm rondelle on cords 7 and 8 (the center cords) **[j]**.

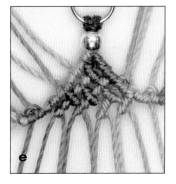

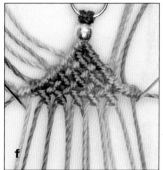

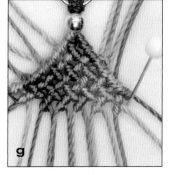

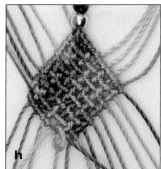

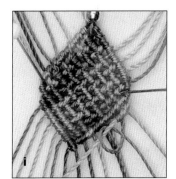

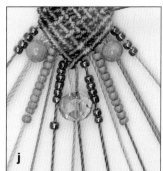

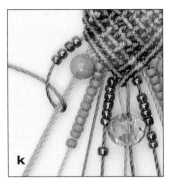

k

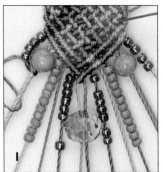

l

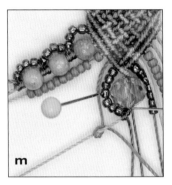

m

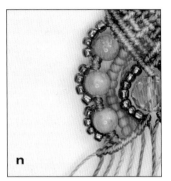

n

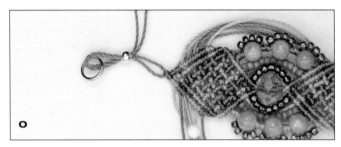

o

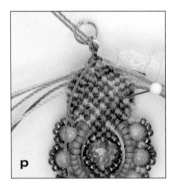

p

q

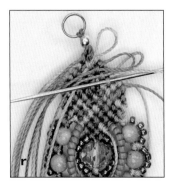

r

Make Side Segments

10 On the left side, use cord 1 to tie a vertical LHk below the 4mm strung on cords 2 and 3. Reverse the order in which you tie this knot. Start the knot by passing cord 1 under and around cords 2 and 3 **[k]**; then on the next part of the knot, pass cord 1 over and around the holding cords **[l]**.

11 For the next segment, string four As on cord 1 and a 4mm on cords 2 and 3, and tie another vertical LHk under the 4mm. Repeat for a total of three segments.

12 Repeat the three segments on the right side with cords 12–14.

13 Enclose the beads with diagonal DHHk rows from the center outward **[m, n]**.

When creating the lines of diagonal DHHk, the beads strung on the cords determine the lengths of those segments. But when the cords have no beads, you may end up with a segment that is too short or too long. Place a pin in the middle of these cords as a measuring point, and then tie the DHHk.

14 Create a diamond shape: For a 6–6.5" (15–16.5cm) wrist, you'll need five diamond shapes in total; for a 7" (18cm) wrist, you'll need six.

15 On the two central cords, string an 8º metal seed bead and the other split ring, and then pass both cords through the 8º again **[o]**. Adjust the cords, bringing the ends to the back so the bead and the ring are close to the work **[p]**. Apply a dot of superglue to the bottom of the 8º, and let dry.

16 Secure the cords on the back of the piece. Pay special attention to the two center cords, making sure that they are well secured. Thread the cords on an embroidery needle and pass them through the knots on the back of the work **[q, r]**. Leave a small loop, and apply fabric glue to the cords before pulling them through to secure them. Apply another coat of glue, wait for the glue to dry, and then cut off the excess cords.

17 Fasten the ends, if necessary, on the other end of the bracelet.

18 Add a jump ring and the clasp on one end, and add a jump ring and the extension chain on the other (Basics, p. 19).

Lovely Cycle
Bracelet

In this project, you will learn how to make a micro-macramé wheel that becomes a unique style of clasp and the focal point of the piece at the same time. Faceted fire-polished beads and metal seed beads throughout the piece give the cords an unexpected sheen.

MATERIALS & TOOLS
- fray check
- fabric glue
- scissors
- macramé board and pins

Wheel
- 0.5mm nylon cords
    4 35" (89cm), color A–D
    35", color E
- **36** 11º seed beads in each of colors A and B
- **12** 8º metal seed beads
- **12** 3mm faceted fire-polished beads

Bracelet
- **7** 70" (1.78m) 0.5mm nylon cords, color F
- less than 1g 11º seed beads in each of **2** colors: A, B
- 32mm toggle bar

Material notes
Use nylon cord such as C-Lon beading cord, or S-Lon cord #18. For the body of the wheel (cords A–D), choose four different colors. For the color E cord, chose a similar color as the cord used for the middle of the wheel (refer to "Mount the cords," p. 74).

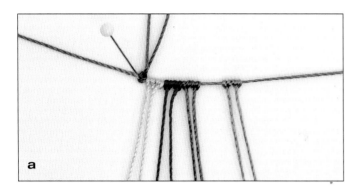

a

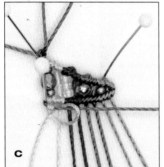

b

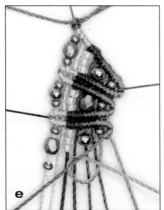

c

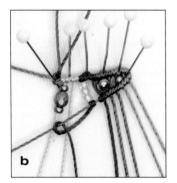

d

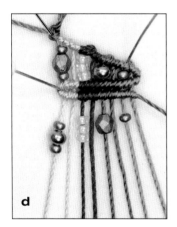

e

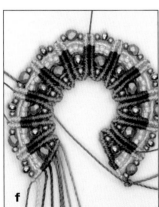

f

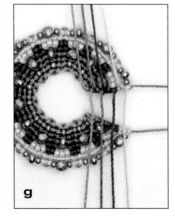

g

Mount the Cords

1 Using the color E cord, make a slip knot, leaving a 10" (25cm) tail. Pin the knot onto the board. This is the runner cord.

2 Attach the color A–D cords over the runner cord, folding them in half and using a reverse lark's head knot (LHk) with half-hitch. From left to right, start with the cord you have chosen to be on the exterior part of the wheel **[a]**.

3 Pin the mounted cords horizontally.

Make the Triangle Shapes

4 Number the cords from 1–8, from left to right. (You may want to reposition the piece as you are knotting, as it will take on a round shape.)

5 String the beads.
Cord 1: a color A 11º seed bead, a 3mm bead, and an A 11º.
Cord 3: three color B 11º seed beads.
Cord 5: an 8º seed bead.
Cord 7: an A 11º.

The bigger the beads you use on the edges, the less DHHk rows you will need to tie for the wheel to join. Keep this in mind if you decide to use different-sized beads.

6 Place a pin to the left of the runner cord so your next

row of double half-hitch knots (DHHk) is straight. Enclose the beads by taking the right end of the runner cord as the holding cord and tying a row of DHHk from right to left **[b]**.

7 Place a pin to the right of the runner cord and bring it back to the right to create another row of DHHk below the previous one **[c]**.

8 String beads as in step 5. Switch the 3mm on cord 1 with the 8º on cord 5 **[d]**.

9 Repeat steps 6–8, alternating the strung beads **[e]**, until you have 12 triangular beaded sections.

10 Tie a row of DHHk to enclose the beads **[f]**.

Close the Wheel

11 Turn the piece over. Place the ends of the runner cords to your right side, then number the knotting cords from 1–8 (from left to right).

12 Set aside cords 1, 3, 5, and 7. Thread cord 2 on an embroidery needle, and pass the cord through the back part of the mounted cord of the same color. Repeat with cords 4, 6, and 8 **[g]**. Pull these cords to close the wheel.

13 Position the working cords to hang vertically. Release the slip knot made in step 1 on the runner cord, and using the upper end as the holding cord, make a row

of DHHk with all eight hanging cords from right to left **[h]**. Adjust the knots so both ends of the piece join without leaving any space in between.

14 Bring the end of the runner cord back to the right, making a short row of five DHHk **[i]**.

15 Using the other end of the runner cord (which is to the right) as the holding cord, make a row of three DHHk toward the left. Both ends of the runner cords have met **[j]**.

16 Apply fabric glue to the back of these last knotted rows, let the glue dry **[k]**, and cut the excess cords except for the two ends of the runner cord.

Add the Bracelet Cords

17 Pin the piece to the board. Using both ends of the runner cord as the mounting cords, attach the seven 70" (1.78m) cords, folding them in half and using reverse LHk with half-hitch. Make sure they are mounted facing the right side **[l]**.

18 Thread the end of a mounting cord (previously called runner cords) through an embroidery needle and leaving three triangular motifs in between, pass through the back knots of the second color in the wheel, starting from the outer edge **[m]**. Repeat with the remaining mounting

cords one at a time, passing each cord through a different back knot to avoid deforming the knots in the front. Secure these ends using a square knot (SQk). (This knot will not have filler cords.) Tighten and apply fabric glue to the SQk to keep it tied.

19 Working on the front, fold and pin the bottom part of the wheel over the mounted cords to get this part out of the way. Pin the mounted cords to the board horizontally.

Make the Knotted Pattern

At this point, you have 14 working cords and two holding cords coming from the wheel. Set the holding cords aside and pair off the 14 working cords. As you work through the pattern, use the left cord of each pair as the holding cord to tie the left-sided half-hitch. The pattern tends to grow diagonally because it uses the rightmost cord as the holding cord for all rows. Make two rows to even the pattern:

20 Number the cords from 1–14 (from left to right). Make four pairs with cords 1–8. (The left cord of each pair is the holding cord.) Using the leftmost pair, make four half-hitches; using the next pair, THHk; using the pair that follows, a DHHk; and using the last pair, a half-hitch **[n]**.

h

i

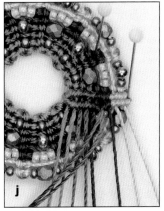

j

k

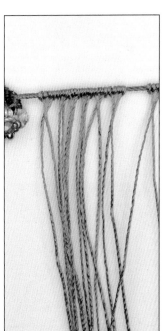

l

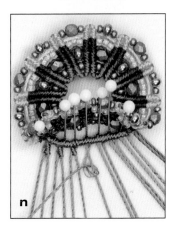

m

n

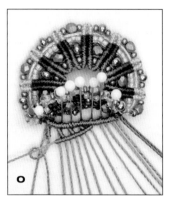

o

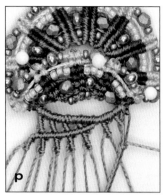

p

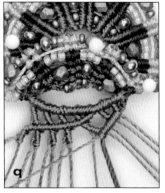

q

r

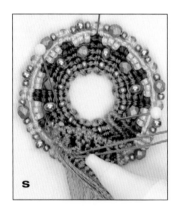

s

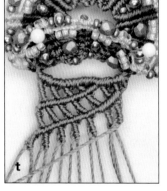

t

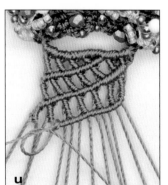

u

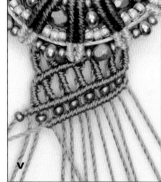

v

21 Re-number the cords from left to right. Using cord 10 as the holding cord, create a diagonal row of nine DHHk toward the left **[o]**.

22 Pair the remaining working cords for a total of seven pairs. Starting with the first five pairs on the left side, tie four half-hitches with each pair; with the next pair, a THHk; on the last pair, a DHHk **[p]**.

23 Re-number the cords. Using cord 14 and both of the mounting cords to the right as the holding cords, tie a row of DHHk with the next four cords from right to left. Release the mounting cords **[q]**, and continue the row with only one holding cord with the next nine cords to the left **[r]**. The first part of this row will look thicker than the rest, but the wheel will cover it. Bring the leftover cords to the back. To secure these cords, apply fabric glue onto the back of the DHHk where they have passed **[s]**. Let the glue dry, and then trim the excess cord.

24 Pair the cords again, and repeat the four left-sided half-hitch across the row with each pair **[t]**.

25 Using the rightmost cord as the holding cord, make a row of DHHk toward the left with the next 13 cords **[u]**.

26 Re-number the cords, and string an 11º seed bead on the odd-numbered cords (1, 3, 5, 7, 9, 11, and 13). Enclose the beads with a DHHk, using cord 14 as the holding cord and knotting toward the left **[v]**.

27 Repeat steps 24 and 25 twice and step 26 once, until you reach the desired length **[w]** (evening the bracelet end and adding the toggle bar adds approximately ¾–1"/ 1.9–2.5cm to the overall length).

28 To even the other end of the bracelet, on the last row of the pattern, make half-hitch on six of the pairs of cords, increasing the number of knots across the row from left to right. Skip the first pair of cords to the left; on the second pair, make a half-hitch, on the third a DHHk, and so on **[x]**. You may need to add more half-hitches on the last rows to the right if the row is still uneven.

29 Cross cords 1 and 14. Using them as holding cords, create a horizontal row of DHHk, using the remaining cords between them (Basics, p. 16) **[y, z]**. Don't adjust the knots too much.

Add the Toggle Bar

30 Working on the back, from left to right, pass cords 6, 7, and 8 through the ring on the toggle bar. Fold two of these cords over toward the work, thread them through an embroidery needle, and pass them through the knots on the back of the last row of DHHk, leaving a small distance of about ⅜" (10mm) from the toggle bar **[aa, bb]**. This keeps the cords in place while you work on the following step.

31 Turn the piece to the front. Use the third cord to tie an alternating DHHk over the folded cords. Starting from the toggle bar toward the piece, tie the knots to cover the distance left from the working piece to the toggle bar **[cc]**.

Finishing

32 Flip the work over. Take the first cord on the left as the holding cord to create a horizontal row of DHHk using the next six cords from the left to the center. Repeat, using the last cord as the holding cord and working from the right to the center **[dd]**.

33 Make a SQk to secure both holding cords in the middle.

34 Apply fabric glue to the last rows of DHHk and the SQk on the back. Let dry, and cut the excess cords.

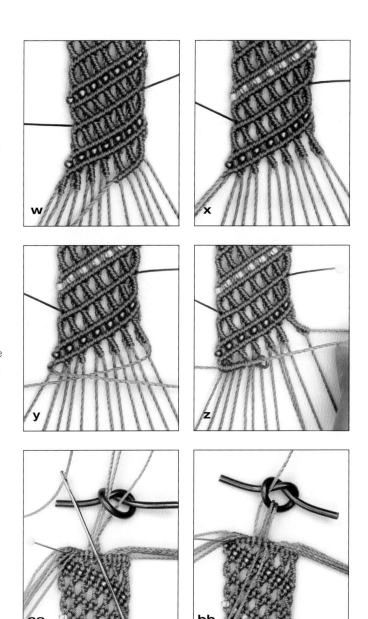

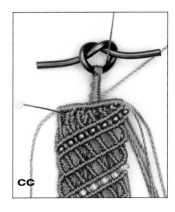

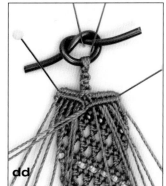

Wrapped Aztec Treasure
Bracelet

I love this modern take on traditional Aztec-style jewelry. The deep adobe color and creamy glass pearls throughout the bracelet complete the overall look. Using micro-macramé to create a bezel around the glass button will help the focal stand out.

MATERIALS & TOOLS

- 0.5mm nylon cords
  - **2** 20" (51cm)
  - 80" (2.03m)
  - **16** 40" (1m)
  - **4** 50" (1.27m)
  - 50" different color
- approximately 28x4mm glass button
- 1g 11⁰ seed beads
- **4** 8mm wide-hole glass pearls
- **2** 6mm cord end beads
- 6" (15cm) piece of waxed cardboard, ⁵/₁₆ wide
- masking tape
- embroidery needle

- scissors
- macramé board and pins
- embroidery needle
- superglue
- fabric glue
- wire cutters (optional)
- macramé board and pins

Material notes

Use 0.5mm nylon cord such as C-Lon beading cord or Tuff cord #5. The 8mm glass pearls should fit at least three cords; the 6mm end beads hole should fit six. You can substitute a cabochon or stone for the glass button. A piece of cardboard maintains an even separation between the knots on each side of the knotted bezel. Waxed cardboard (such as cups at fast food restaurants, for example) is easier to remove when you're finished. The cardboard should be about 4mm more than the thickness of your button, cabochon, or stone.

Make the Knotted Bezel

First, make a knotted bezel to hold the button.

1 Using the 20" (51cm) cords and the 80" (2.03m) cord, and leaving about 5" (13cm) at one end, make a slip knot with the cords. Pin the knot to the board, and place and center the cardboard below. Place a pin on each side of the cardboard right where the chain will begin **[a]**.

2 To start knotting the chain, pass the longest cord underneath the cardboard to the opposite side to tie a vertical lark's head knot (LHk) that faces the center, over the left cord **[b]**. Adjust the knot next to the pin. The longest cord is the knotting cord. The other two cords are holding cords.

> Tighten the knotting cord gently before making the next knot so that it doesn't loosen. The knots should have the same amount of tension.

3 Pass the knotting cord over the cardboard to the opposite side, and on the right holding cord, make a vertical LHk facing the center **[c]**. Adjust the knot.

4 Repeat steps 2 and 3 until you reach the desired length. Remember, the knotting cord passes beneath the cardboard and the next time,

it passes over the cardboard. The last knot in the chain will be on the side where the first knot was made **[d]**.

> If the cardboard lifts up, secure it to the board with a piece of masking tape, leaving a small section on the bottom of the cardboard to lift it when you need to pass the cord underneath.

5 Check the bezel size. There should be enough space to adjust the holding cords so the button fits inside the bezel **[e]**. (I made 37 vertical LHks on the right side of the bezel. Either face of this chain can be used in the front of the project.)

Wrap the Button

6 Remove the piece of cardboard between the knots. Place the two ends of the knotting cord toward the back of the button. Adjust and tie the ends of the holding cord with a square knot (SQk) in the front **[f]**, and do the same with the holding cord ends in back. The SQk doesn't have filler cords.

a

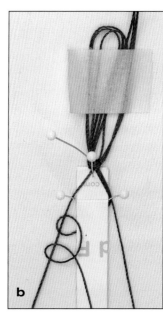

b

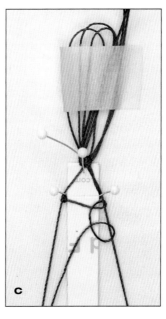

c

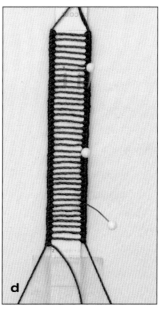

d

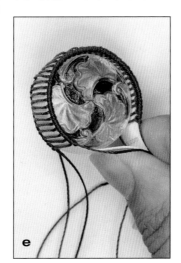

e

f

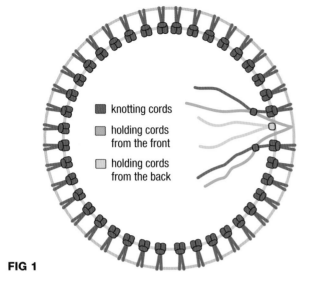

FIG 1

knotting cords

holding cords from the front

holding cords from the back

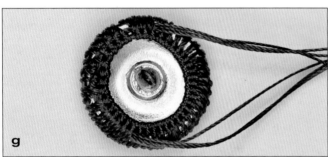

g

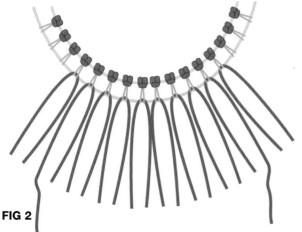

h

i

FIG 2

7 Pass the front holding cords to the back of the button. Use each front holding cord to tie a SQk with one of the holding cords from the back of the button as shown in **FIG 1**. With the six cords now at the back, pass the three cords from one side to the other through the chain on the back using an embroidery needle. Do this in the opposite direction with the remaining three cords **[g]**.

8 Arrange the knots so they are evenly distributed around the button.

Add the Hanging Cords

9 Using an embroidery needle, thread eight 40" (1m) cords and two 50" (1.27m) cords through the edges of the button, one by one. Pass the cords through the two cords that make up a LHk on the back of the button **[h, i]**.

10 Add cords in the following order: a 40" (1m) cord, a 50" (1.27m)

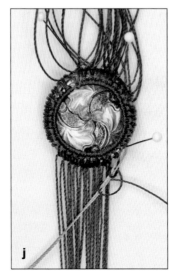

j

cord, six 40" cords, a 50" cord, and a 40" cord.

11 Slide the cords to the edge of the button, and even the ends of the short cords so they are the same length on each side. When you arrange the 50" cords, one end should measure 30" (76cm). Place the longer ends in the 3rd and 18th position **[FIG 2]**.

12 Repeat the previous steps to attach the cords on the other side of the button, leaving an even space without cords on each side of the button.

Add the Main Holding Cord

Place the piece so the hanging cords from one half hang vertically toward you.

13 Fold the same or a different color 50" cord in half, and leaving a small loop, pin it on the right side of the hanging cords **[j]**. The two ends become the main holding cords.

14 Using the holding cords together, make a row of DHHk with all the hanging cords surrounding the button, from right to left **[k]**.

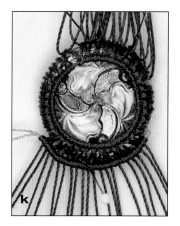

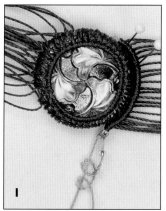

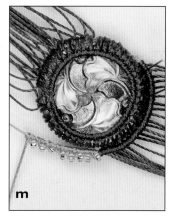

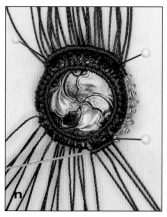

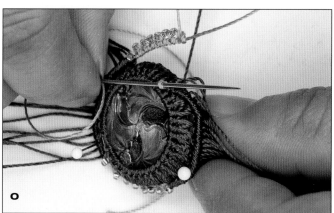

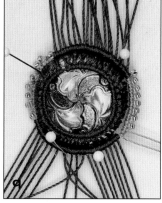

Mark the main holding cords if you have decided to use the same color as the rest of the cords: Paint it with a marker or make a slip knot on the end.

The hanging cords are not secure, so when one of the cords' ends is to be knotted, the cord could shift. To prevent this, place a piece of masking tape and a pin on the end that will not be knotted yet. Knot with the first end, and then remove the pin and the tape to knot the other end. Adjust it and ensure that it is as close as possible to the first knot and to the button.

Knot on the Edges

15 Using the two main holding cords that are now on the left, add an 11º seed bead on one end and, using the other as the holding cord, make a right-sided vertical LHk (make the knot under and around the holding cord first, then over and around it) **[l]**. Repeat these steps until you have a chain that reaches the other side of the bracelet (approximately eight or nine times). The main holding cords have reached the opposite side **[m, n]**.

Work on the Opposite Side

16 Turn the piece to the other side and repeat steps 14 and 15.

17 Using the colored holding cords next to the loop

formed when it was mounted, pass one end through the loop to join them **[o]**. Arrange and distribute the knots so that the work is symmetrical.

18 Secure the six cords on the back of the button that were left hanging. Apply a generous amount of fabric glue on the cords where they pass through **[p]**. Let dry, and cut off the excess cords.

Return to the First Side

19 Arrange the piece again so that the ends of the main holding cords are on the right-hand side. Divide the hanging cords into three groups: seven cords on the left, five in the middle, and eight on the right.

Work with the Central Five Cords

20 Using the two cords that are furthest to the left and one cord that is furthest to the right in this group, cross them over and use them as holding cords to make a horizontal THHk with each of the two cords left in between **[q]**. Pull the crossed ends and adjust the cords.

21 String an 8mm pearl on the two cords that were used to tie the THHk.

Enclose the First Pearl

22 You should have 10 cords to the right of the pearl. Use the main holding cords to make a DHHk row with nine cords from right to left. The last knotting cord becomes a holding cord. Holding the three holding cords together, use the next cord to the left as the knotting cord to make a chain of six alternating DHHk (start the chain with a right-sided DHHk) **[r]**. This thread also becomes a holding cord, which makes a total of four holding cords.

> To count alternating DHHk, look at the ridges that form as you switch the knotting cord from one side to the other. If you use pins, count the pins and add one that corresponds to the last knot where the chain ends.

23 Pin the end of the alternating DHHk chain by the hole of the pearl to frame it. Using one of the cords coming out of the bead, make a DHHk over the four holding cords. Then release the longer of the last two added holding cords. Using the other cord

exiting the bead, make another DHHk **[s]**. You will now have three cords in the center and three holding cords.

24 Rotate the work slightly to the left. Use a holding cord the same color as the rest of the bracelet. Use the knotting cord to make a chain of six alternating DHHk to enclose the pearl. Knot toward the opposite side of the bead first (right-sided knot) **[t]**. After that, you will not be using this knotting cord anymore. Thread it through an embroidery needle and firmly secure the cord through the back of the piece, while the newly formed chain encloses the bead in the front **[u]**. Apply fabric glue. Let it dry thoroughly and cut the excess cord.

25 Turn the work back over to the front and, using the main holding cords, continue tying DHHk using the eight remaining cords to the left **[v]**. Pass the ends of the main holding cord through the knots on the back of the button, so they exit beside the LHk chain on the opposite side **[w]**.

Alternating DHHk Chains Around the First Pearl

26 For these chains, use only the three cords next to the bead on the left and right sides. Number the cords on both sides separately from 1–3, from left to right. On the left side, using cords 1 and 2 as the holding cords and cord 3 as the knotting cord, make nine

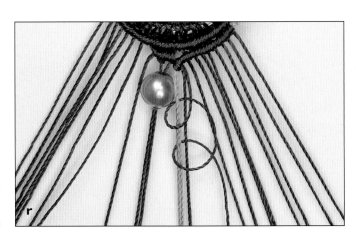

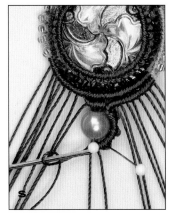

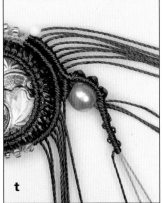

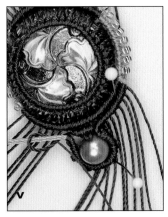

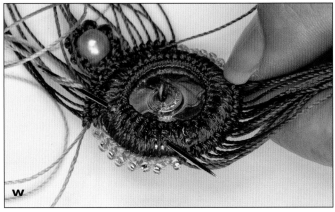

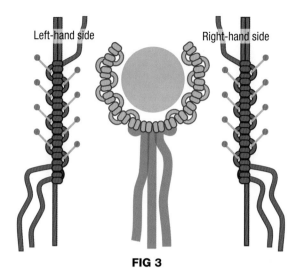

Left-hand side   Right-hand side

FIG 3

alternating DHHk. Start and finish this chain with a left-sided DHHk **[FIG 3]**. Release the knotting cord (cord 3), then take one of the two holding cords to make a left-sided DHHk over the other holding cord. Both knotted cords should end toward the left.

27 Repeat with the chain on the right side. Using cord 1 as the knotting cord and cords 2 and 3 as the holding cords, tie a chain of nine alternating DHHk. Start and finish this chain with a right-sided DHHk. Release the knotting cord (cord 1), then use one of the holding cords to make a right-sided DHHk over the other holding cord. Both knotted cords should end to the right.

28 Make sure the chains of alternating DHHk on both sides of the bead are the same length. Cross the chains' holding cords to tie DHHk using the three cords that hang under

the bead in the middle **[x]**. Use pins to keep the chains as close as possible to the bead. Adjust by pulling the holding cords **[y]**.

Add the Second Pearl

29 Insert another bead in the three center cords. Mark the left or right cord, which is coming from the first pearl. Keep at least one there to secure the first bead.

30 Apply glue to the section where the second bead will be resting and then slide it into place **[z]**. Wait for it to dry completely, and cut the two cords that were not marked. For extra security, apply fabric glue to the back of the DHHk above the second bead **[aa]**.

31 Number the three cords on each side of the second bead separately from 1–3, from left to right. Work with the left cords. Using cord 1 as the knotting cord and the other two cords as holding cords, make a chain of six alternating DHHk, starting the chain with a right-sided DHHk **[bb]**. Use a holding cord as the knotting cord to make a left-sided DHHk over the other one. Both knotting cords are now on the left side **[FIG 4, p. 84]**.

32 On the right side, use cord 3 as the knotting cord and the other two cords as the holding cords to make a chain of six alternating

x

y

z

aa

bb

FIG 4

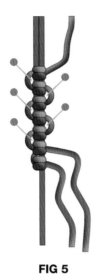

FIG 5

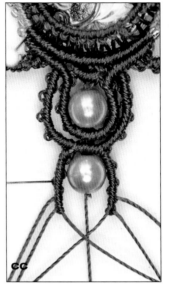

cc

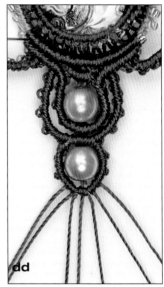

dd

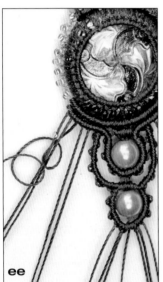

ee

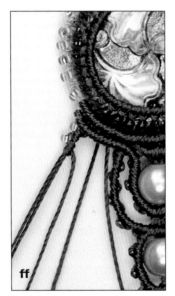

ff

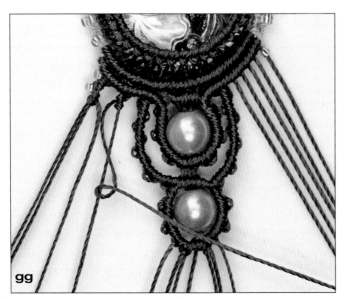

gg

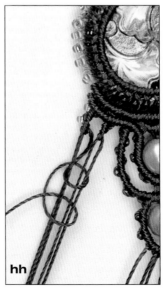

hh

DHHk, starting the chain with a left-sided DHHk. Then take one of the holding cords as the knotting cord to make a right-sided DHHk over the other one. Both knotting cords are now on the right side **[FIG 5]**.

33 Pin one of these chains close to the pearl, cross both holding cords coming from the chains, and then tie a DHHk, using the cord out of the pearl **[cc]**. Adjust by pulling the holding cords **[dd]**.

Alternating DHHk Chains on the Outsides

34 Number the five left-most cords from 1–5, from left to right. String an 11º seed bead on cord 1, and then use cord 3 (the longer cord on the left-hand side) as the knotting cord to tie a left-sided DHHk over cords 1 and 2 together **[ee]**. Add an 11º to the knotting cord, and make a right-sided DHHk over the two holding cords **[ff]**.

35 Use cord 4 as the holding cord and cord 5 as the knotting cord to make a left-sided DHHk and a right-sided half-hitch **[gg]**.

36 Take the knotting cord (the longer cord) in the first group, and pass it to the left under the holding cords. Tie a left-sided DHHk using the remaining four cords as the holding cords **[hh]**. Add an 11º to the knotting cord and following the sequence

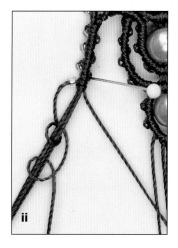

ii

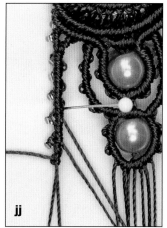

jj

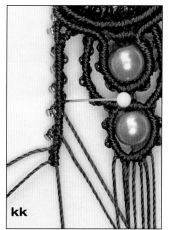

kk

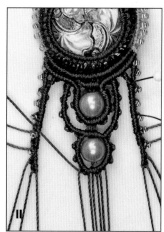

ll

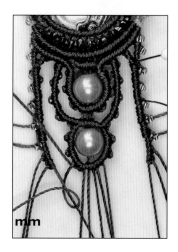

mm

on the alternating DHHk chain, continue knotting until you have added a total of five 11ºs (only add 11ºs when the knotting cord is outward on the left side).

37 Decrease two holding cords after you have strung the next two 11ºs. When you have strung the sixth 11º in the alternating DHHk chain, decrease a holding cord by setting one of them aside to the right **[ii]**. Continue knotting one right-sided and one left-sided DHHk over the remaining three holding cords. Add the next 11º on the knotting cord, and decrease again, separating another holding cord to the right **[jj]**. Make a right-sided DHHk and a left-sided half-hitch so the knotting cord is in that direction. Use masking tape to keep the two cords that have been set aside out of the way. They will not be used anymore. To finish this section, use a remaining holding cords in the alternating DHHk chain to make a left-sided DHHk over the other holding cord **[kk]**.

38 Number the five right-most cords from 1–5, from left to right, and begin making a mirror image of the first section: Using cord 1 as the knotting cord and cord 2 as the holding cord, make a right-sided DHHk and a left-sided half-hitch.

39 Make a chain of alternating DHHk using cords 3–5. String an 11º on cord 5. Using cord 3 (the longer cord in the right-hand side) as the knotting cord, tie a right-sided DHHk over cords 4 and 5 together. Next, add another 11º on the knotting cord, and make a left-sided DHHk over the two holding cords.

40 Tie an alternating DHHk chain using cords 1–5. Take the knotting cord (the longer cord) in the second group, and pass it to the right under the holding cords. Tie a right-sided DHHk using the remaining four cords as the holding cords. Add another 11º on the knotting cord and,

following the sequence on the alternating DHHk chain, continue knotting until you have added a total of five 11ºs.

41 Decrease two holding cords after you have strung the next two 11ºs. When you have strung the sixth 11º in the alternating DHHk chain, decrease a holding cord by setting one of them aside to the left. Continue knotting a left-sided and a right-sided DHHk over the remaining three holding cords. Add the next 11º on the knotting cord, and decrease again, separating another holding cord to the left. Make a left-sided DHHk and a right-sided half-hitch so the knotting cord is in that direction. Use masking tape to keep the two cords that have been set aside out of the way. Use one of the remaining holding cords in the alternating DHHk chain to make a right-sided DHHk over the other holding cord.

Narrow the Ends

42 Release one of the seven central cords

underneath the pearl (I let go of the second cord) **[ll]**. Number the remaining 12 cords from left to right.

43 **Row 1:** Using cord 3 as the holding cord (this is the holding cord from the left alternating DHHk chain), make a row of DHHk using cords 4, 5, and 6 **[mm]**. Re-number the cords. On the right side, use cord 10 as the holding cord (this is also the holding cord from the right alternating DHHk chain) to tie a row of four DHHk to the left. Note that the left rows of DHHk use one less cord than the right rows.

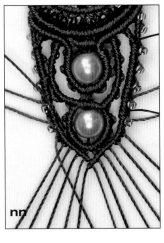

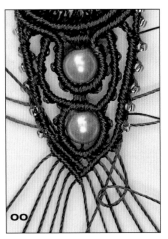

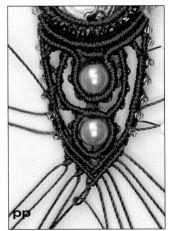

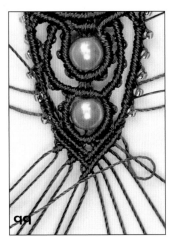

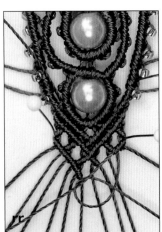

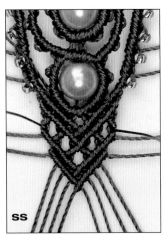

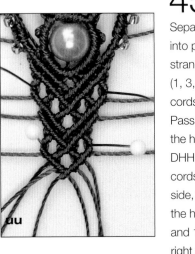

44 **Row 2:** Re-number the cords and create a second row of DHHk below the first one. Using cord 1 as the holding cord, and knotting to the center, make five DHHk **[nn]**. Repeat on the right side, using cord 12 as the holding cord, to make six DHHk toward the middle **[oo]**.

45 **Row 3 (openwork):** Re-number the cords. Separate the six left cords into pairs. In each pair, the left strands are the knotting cords (1, 3, and 5), and the right cords are the holding cords. Pass the knotting cord under the holding cord to make a DHHk with each pair of cords **[pp]**. On the right-hand side, the cords on the left are the holding cords (cords 7, 9, and 11), while the cords on the right are the knotting cords. Make a DHHk with each pair **[qq]**.

46 **Row 4:** Use a pin at the beginning of these rows to keep the lines straight. Using cord 1 as the holding cord, knot to the center and make five DHHk. Repeat on the right side, using cord 12 as the holding cord to make six DHHk to the center **[rr]**. Decrease the number of cords more by ignoring cords 1 and 12.

47 **Row 5:** Re-number the remaining cords from 1–10. Use cord 1 as the holding cord, and tie a second row of four DHHk toward the center. On the right side, use cord 10 as the holding cord to make five DHHk to the center. Decrease again, ignoring cords 1 and 10 **[ss]**.

48 **Row 6 (openwork):** Separate the remaining eight cords into pairs. Knot as you did in row 3, only here, you have fewer cords.

49 **Row 7:** Re-number the cords and make a row of three DHHk using cord 1 as the holding cord, from left to the center **[tt]**. Repeat on the right side, using cord 8 as the holding cord, to make four DHHk to the center **[uu]**. Decrease, ignoring cords 1 and 8.

50 **Row 8:** Using the remaining six cords, make accumulating knots, using cord 1 as the holding cord and ending in the middle **[vv]**. Repeat on the right side, in the opposite direction, using cord 6 as the holding cord **[ww]**.

51 Once the two bundles of cords are in the center, take any one of the knotting cords to make a single bundle with a DHHk **[xx]**.

52 Repeat from step 19 on the other side of the bracelet.

53 Working on the back, secure all the cords: One at a time, thread the cords onto an embroidery needle and pass them through some of the knots on the back **[yy]**. Apply fabric glue to the knots and to the ends of the cords. Make sure the glue does not come through to the front of the work. Let the glue dry, and cut the excess cords.

54 Braid the six cords on each end, and make a sliding knot clasp (Basics, p. 18).

55 Leave the button's shank as is, or crush it a bit without leaving corners that would poke the skin. You can also use wire cutters to cut it off, making sure that there are no edges that will scrape the skin, and then cover the area with a round piece of fabric like suede, Ultrasuede, or felt, using E6000 adhesive.

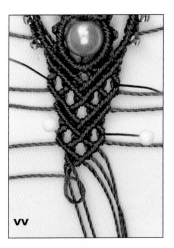

vv

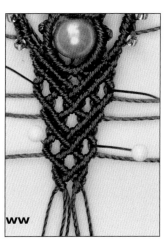

ww

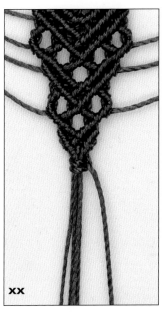

xx

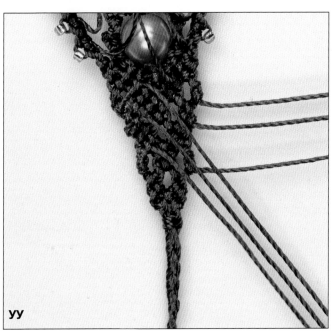

yy

Colorful Flower
Brooch

You'll enjoy learning how to make this gorgeous, multipurpose flower. The flower is made with alternating double half-hitch knot chains. Alternating the length or adding more cords creates different effects and sizes. Mount your flower on a hair clip or on a ring, or create a bold and beautiful necklace with several flowers in different sizes.

MATERIALS & TOOLS
- 0.5mm nylon cords
    - 65" (1.65m), color A
    - 50" (1.27), color B
    - 75" (1.91m), color C
    - 10' (3.05m), color D
- superglue
- fabric glue
- 25mm brooch clasp
- scissors
- macramé board and pins

Material notes
Use nylon cord such as C-Lon beading cord, or S-Lon cord #18. Color A is used for the mounting cord and to make a chain in the central part of the flower. The remaining cords are identified starting with the cord closest to the center of the flower.

Make the Flower

1 Using the color A cord, make a slip knot, leaving a 10" (25cm) tail. Pin the knot to the board.

2 Fold the color B cord in half, the color C cord with the right end measuring 25" (64cm), and color D cord in half. Attach the cords over cord A from right to left using lark's head knot (LHk) with half-hitches. The rightmost cords will be closer to the center of the flower **[a]**.

3 Pin the mounted cords horizontally. Using the rightmost cord as the holding cord, tie a row of four double half-hitch knots (DHHk) to the left **[b]**.

4 Using the rightmost cord as the holding cord, tie a line of two DHHk below the previous row, from right to left **[c]**. Reposition and pin the piece so the DHHk rows are placed vertically.

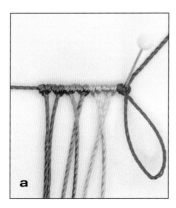

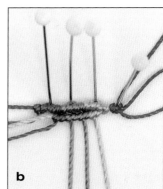

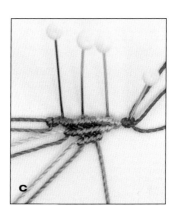

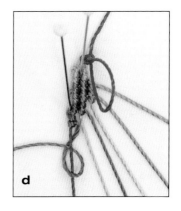

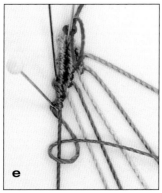

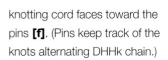

5 From left to right, create three alternating DHHk chains of different lengths, using two cords for each. For the first chain, take the two leftmost cords and using the same holding cord (coming from the mounting line), tie a left-sided DHHk with the other cord **[d]**. Then, place a pin to the left of the holding cord and under the knotting cord, and tie a right-sided DHHk **[e]**.

6 Make an alternating DHHk chain until you have placed seven pins to the left of the chain. Under the seventh pin, make a right-sided DHHk, then a left-sided half-hitch so the

knotting cord faces toward the pins **[f]**. (Pins keep track of the knots alternating DHHk chain.)

7 For the second and third chains, repeat this step using the next pairs of cords. For each chain, use the holding cords coming from the rows of

DHHk made before on steps 3 and 4. Start and finish each chain in the exact same way as the first one. The difference is that you will only place five pins to the left of the second chain **[g, h]** and three pins on the third chain **[i, j]**. Reposition the piece horizontally.

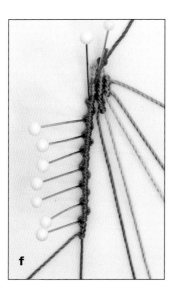

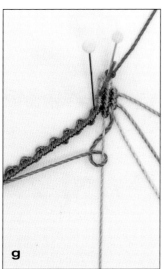

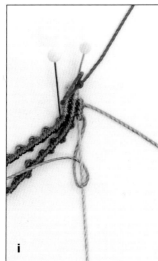

8 Fold the shortest chain **[k]**, placing its holding cord next to the cord that is hanging to the right **[l]**, and use this cord to tie a DHHk over the holding cord coming from the chain **[m]**.

9 Fold the second chain next to the three cords that are now hanging to the right **[n]** and make three DHHk using those cords **[o]**.

10 Fold the remaining chain in half, placing its holding cord next to the hanging cords on the right. Make two accumulating knots (Basics, p. 14) from left to right. Start by taking the two cords, from the chain, together as the holding cords, and tie a DHHk with the next cord, from left to right **[p]**, place this last knotting cord with the holding cords; repeat with the next cord **[q]**. After that, keep making DHHk with the next cords, but you will release these after completing the knot. You will now have three hanging cords

and a bundle of four holding cords **[r]**.

11 Central alternating DHHk chain: Take cord A from the bundled cords, to tie a chain of five alternating DHHk over the remaining cords in the bundle. Start and finish with a right-sided DHHk **[s, t]**.

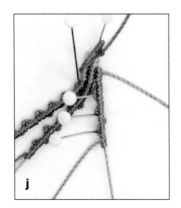

j

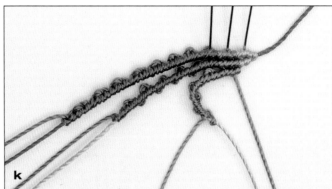

k

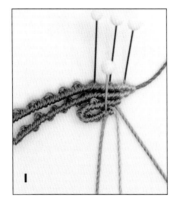

l

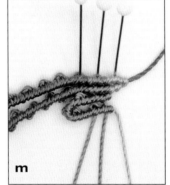

m

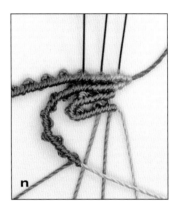

n

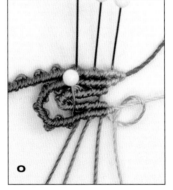

o

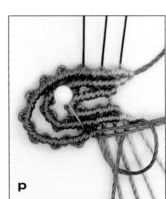

p

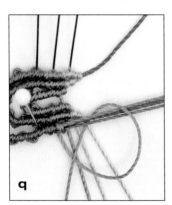

q

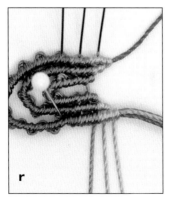

r

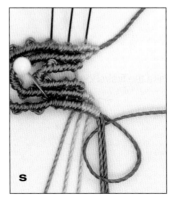

s

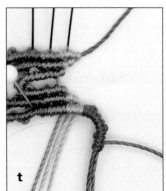

t

Fold this chain to the left and, taking the four cords from it as the holding cords, tie a row of three DHHk row using the cords to the left **[u, v]**.

12 One by one, release the cords from the bundle. Start by taking the cord that matches the color of the last knotted cord to make a DHHk over the rest of the bundled cords **[w]** and release it. Repeat with the remaining two cords. The final holding cord is cord A **[x]**.

13 The cords are now in the same position as they were at the beginning of the work. Repeat from step 4 to create more petals **[y],** with a small change to step 11: After the first petal, use cord A from the bundled cords to tie one right-sided DHHk over the remaining cords in the bundle. Then thread this knotting cord onto an embroidery needle and pass it through the last loop formed onto the first central chain **[z]**. Following the sequence, tie four more alternating DHHk over the bundled cords **[aa]**. Repeat steps 4–13 to create four more petals. For the last petal, stop at step 10 and then tie a right-sided DHHk using cord A over the bundled cords.

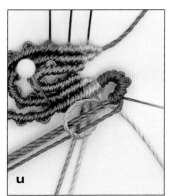
u

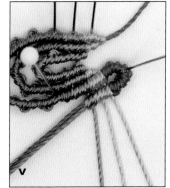
v

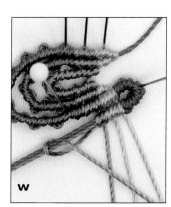
w

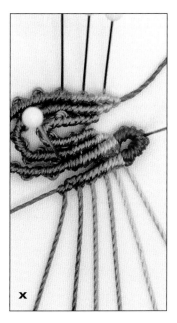
x

y

z

14 After the last knotted petal and before making the central alternating DHHk chain, you will place the first end of cord A inside this chain. Here are two options:
Option 1: Set aside one of the cords from the bundle. Next, take the first/short end of cord A and place it parallel to the bundled cords. Of course, this end will run in the opposite direction as the bundled cords **[bb]**. Take these three cords together as the holding cords, and make five alternating

aa

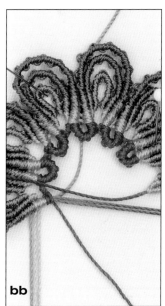
bb

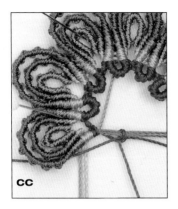
cc

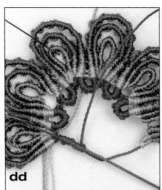
dd

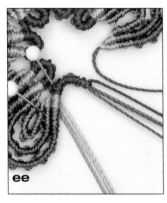
ee

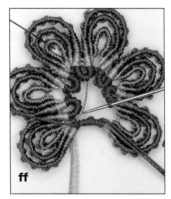
ff

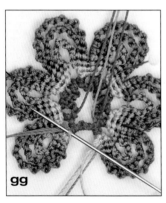
gg

hh

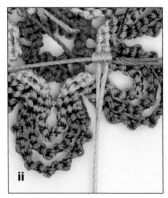
ii

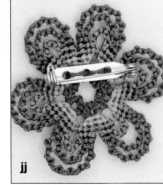
jj

DHHk **[cc]**, as you did before and using the longer end of color A as the knotting cord. Adjust, pulling the short end of color A **[dd]**.

Option 2: Make the alternating DHHk chain as before, but do not adjust the knots too much **[ee]**. Remove one of the cords from the chain so the knots will be even more loose. Set this cord aside. Thread the first end of color A onto an embroidery needle and pass it through the chain in the opposite direction of the holding cords. Pull the short end of color A to adjust.

15 Thread the long end of cord A through an embroidery needle, and pass it through the closest loop in the central alternating DHHk chain of the first petal **[ff]**.

16 Flip the piece to the back. Secure both ends of cord A by passing them through the knots on the back of the work. Place these ends with the cord previously set aside.

17 Join the first and last petals. One by one, thread the three hanging cords from the last petal onto an embroidery needle **[gg]**. Pass each cord through the back part of the mounted cords, matching the color of the cords with the knots on the first petal edge **[hh]**. Pull this cord to close the distance between the first and last petal.

18 Rotate the piece so these cords hang vertically. Cross the two remaining cords from the bundle and the rightmost hanging cord, and tie two DHHk with the cords between them **[ii]**. Make sure these knots are well-tightened so the first and last petals are well joined. (For an easier way to cross the cords and make a DHHk over them, refer to Basics, p. 16.)

19 Due to the laciness of the flower, the brooch clasp may be noticeable from the front. You may paint the side that will face the back of the flower with nail polish and let it dry. Sew on the brooch clasp using one of the leftovers cords. Secure the end of this cord behind the clasp.

20 Apply a generous amount of fabric glue to the knots through which the ends of color A have been passed, on the cord that was set aside, behind the last row of two DHHk that were made to join the petals, and to the cord used to sew the brooch clasp.

21 Let the glue dry, and cut the leftover cords **[jj]**.

Some Ends to It
Bracelet

Combine your favorite beads with two knotted ends to turn them into an interesting but special bracelet. The knotted ends were made with the Cavandoli technique, a variation of macramé used to form geometric patterns like weaving.

MATERIALS & TOOLS
- 0.5mm nylon cords
    - **4** 45" (1.14m)
    - **2** 25" (64cm)
- 14x7mm snap button clasp
- **60** 4–8mm round, flat, oval, and rondelle glass beads
- fabric glue
- hot glue
- scissors
- pair of tweezers
- macramé board and pins

Material note
Use nylon cord as C-Lon beading cord, or S-Lon cord #18. Choose a contrasting color for the 25" (64cm) cords.

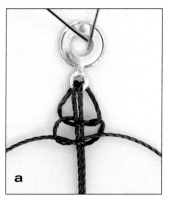

a

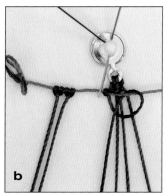

b

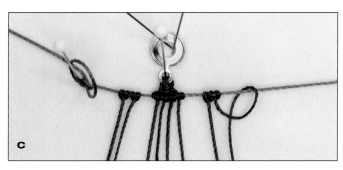

c

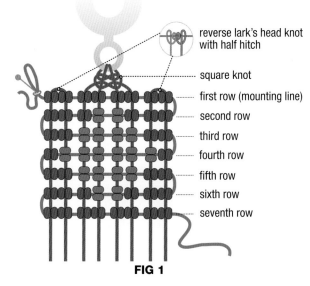

reverse lark's head knot with half hitch

square knot

first row (mounting line)

second row

third row

fourth row

fifth row

sixth row

seventh row

FIG 1

d

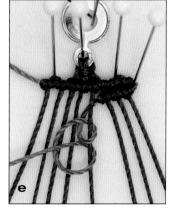

e

Mount the Cords

1 Pass two 45" (1.14m) cords through the loop of the clasp, and center it. Pin the clasp onto the board and, using the back ends of the cords as the knotting cords, tie a square knot over the front ends as the filler cords **[a]**.

2 Make a slip knot about 4" (10cm) from one end of a 25" (64cm) cord, and pin the knot onto the board close from the cords are coming from the clasp. This cord is the *runner cord*.

3 Add the cords over the runner cord from left to right as follows: Fold one of the remaining cords in half, and attach it with a reverse lark's head knot (LHk) with a half-hitch. Next, attach each of the four cords coming from the clasp with a double half-hitch knot (DHHk) **[b]**. Add the remaining cord with a reverse lark's head with half-hitch **[c]**.

First Cavandoli Pattern

The motifs on both ends of this bracelet are knotted using horizontal and vertical DHHk. The runner cord acts as the holding cord for the horizontal DHHk and as the knotting cord for the vertical DHHk **[FIG 1]**.

4 **Row 1:** Slide the cords to the left so they are close together against the slip knot. Pin this line to the board horizontally.

Row 2: Place a pin to the right of the rightmost cord. Using the runner cord as the holding cord to the left, tie three horizontal DHHk **[d]**. Place the runner cord under the next hanging cord to the left, and using the runner cord as the knotting cord, tie two vertical DHHk over the two central cords **[e]**. Finish the row with three horizontal DHHk made over the runner cord **[f, next page]**.

Row 3: Bring the runner cord to the right and tie two horizontal DHHk, four vertical DHHk, and two horizontal DHHk **[see FIG 1]**.

Row 4: Make one horizontal DHHk, six vertical DHHks, and one horizontal DHHk.

Row 5: Repeat the pattern for row 3.

Row 6: Repeat the pattern for row 2.

Row 7: Make a row of eight horizontal DHHk **[g, next page]**.

5 Release the slip knot at the beginning of the runner cord. Thread each end of this cord through an embroidery needle and pass it through the knots on the back of the work **[h, next page]**. Apply fabric glue to the knots. Let the glue dry, and cut the excess runner cords **[i, next page]**.

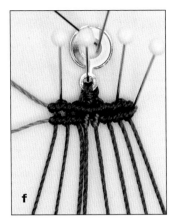

f

g

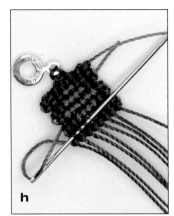

h

i

Make the Beaded Strands

6 Using two cords at a time, string a bead on each pair and tie an overhand knot with both cords. To form the knot where you want it: Make a loose overhand knot under the beads **[j]**. Insert a pair of tweezers through the loop's knot, and grab the cords under the beads at the point where you want the knot **[k]**. While holding the cords in place, pull the cords to tighten the knot. Adjust the knot over the tweezers first **[l]**, pushing the knot into place with your thumbnail. Then remove the tweezers and pull the cords individually.

7 Repeat until the strands reach the desired length **[m]**. On each strand, after stringing the last bead, don't make an overhand knot; make a slip knot.

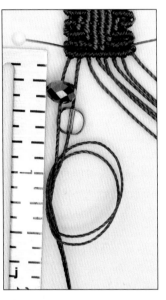

j

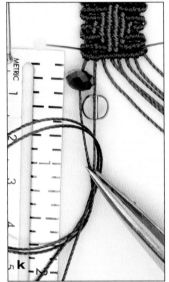

k

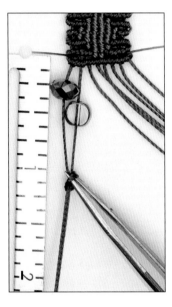

I placed a ruler next to the strands to measure the distance between each overhand knot. This distance can be longer or shorter, depending on your own personal preference and the size of the beads you are using.

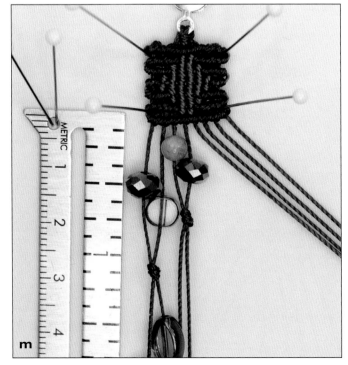

m

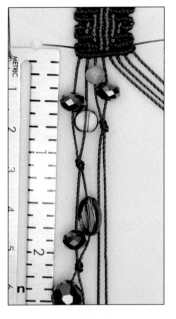

n

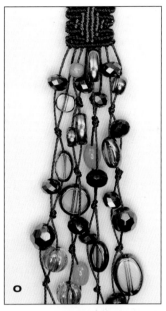

o

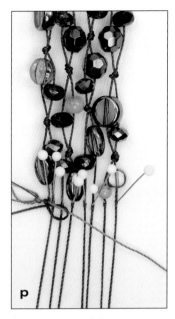

p

Second Cavandoli Pattern

9 Release the slip knots. Pin each cord close together in a horizontal line. This is where the other Cavandoli motif will start.

10 Add the other runner cord. Tie a slip knot on one end, and make a row of eight DHHk over it, using the hanging cords as the knotting cords **[p, q]**.

11 Repeat step 4, rows 2–7, on the other end of the bracelet **[r, s]**.

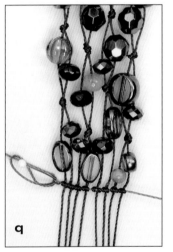

q

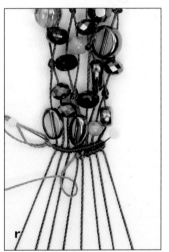

r

s

12 To finish this end, apply fabric glue over the knots where the runner cords have been passed through. Let the glue dry and cut the excess cords, except for the top end of the runner cord **[t]**. Use this end to sew the other part of the clasp onto the back of the Cavandoli motif. The clasp is placed in the middle of the last motif, so when the bracelet is fastened, the ends are as close to each other as possible. Secure the leftover cord **[u]** and apply fabric glue. Let dry and trim.

t

u

8 In the second beaded strand, make the first overhand knot after ½" (1.3cm) so the beads don't bulk up next to each other. After the first knot, tie the knots every 1" (2.5cm) **[n]**. On the third beaded strands, make the first overhand knot after 1". On the fourth beaded strands, make the first knots after ½" **[o]**.

13 Secure the floating section of this side of the clasp using a generous amount of fabric glue or hot glue.

Cavandoli Frames
Bracelet

If you are an expert knotter, this project is definitely for you. This bracelet combines several colors along the rows of vertical double half-hitch knots that form four different patterns. Individual motifs are then mounted on square bezels. I will show you how to carry the cords through the back knots to use when and where you need them so you can change the color according to the pattern.

MATERIALS & TOOLS

- 0.5mm nylon cords
  The diamond
    20" (51cm) color A
    4 15" (38cm) color A
    30" (76cm), color A
    20" (51cm), color B
    20" (51cm), color C
    17" (43cm), color D
  The waves
    2 20" (51cm) color A
    8 15" (38cm) color A
    2 44" (1.12m), color A
    2 17" (43cm), color B
    2 15" (38cm), color C

The arrow
  2 20" (51cm) color A
  8 15" (38cm) color A
  2 38" (97cm), color A
  2 18" (46cm), color B
  2 18" (46cm), color C
  2 12" (30cm) color D
The abstract
  2 20" (51cm) color A
  8 15" (38cm) color A
  2 41" (1.04m) color A
  2 25" (64cm) color B
- adjustable bracelet 18mm square bezels
- E6000 adhesive or Aleene's Jewelry & Metal Glue

- fabric glue
- masking tape
- narrow embroidery needle

- 8" (20cm) ⅝" (15.8mm) thin fabric or ribbon
- flat iron (optional)
- macramé board and pins

Material notes

Make sure your bracelet bezels have an outer diameter of 18mm and an inner work area 17x2mm deep. Use nylon cord such as C-Lon beading cord or #5 Tuff cord in four different colors: A (brown), B (green), C (teal), and D (purple). The motifs for this bracelet are duplicated except for the one in the center, which is called the diamond.

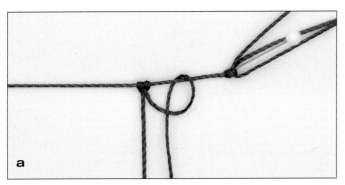

a

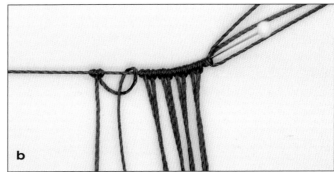

b

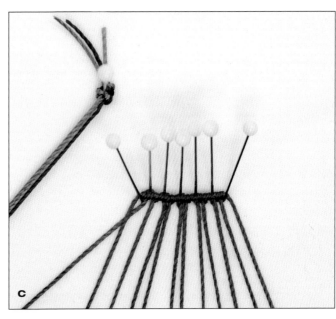

c

Mount the Cords

The seven motifs that make this bracelet will start with the same length and number of cords. Mount the cords in the same way for each of the motifs as shown below.

> Cut the color A holding/knotting cord (see materials list) after you have mounted the cords in this section, so it doesn't get mixed up with these cords that are the same color but different lengths.

1 Use the 20" (51cm) color A cord as the mounting cord and tie a slip knot in the middle of it. Pin the knot to the board.

2 Fold a 15" (38cm) color A cord in half, and attach it over the mounting cord, using a reverse lark's head knot (LHk) with one half-hitch **[a]**: Take the left (or right) end of the cord to tie a half-hitch over the mounting cord. The half-hitch fills up the space in the mounting cord. (If you make another half-hitch with the other end, the cords could exceed the width of the bezel. Attach the other three 15" color A cords the same way.

Add the Holding/ Knotting Cord

The holding/knotting cord is the color A cord you have cut for the motif you are working on. This cord performs two functions: One end will be another holding cord, while the longer end will be the color A knotting cord.

3 Add this cord to the left of the cords mounted before. Fold the holding/knotting cord so one end measures 8" (20cm) (length for the holding cord), and place this short end to the right. Attach the cord over the mounting cord the same way you mounted the other cords **[b]**.

4 Untie the slip knot from step 1 on the mounting cord, and center the mounted cords on it. Each end of the mounting cord will also be a holding cord, for a total of 11 holding cords. Pin the piece to the board, forming a horizontal line with all of the cords hanging vertically. (The second cord from the left is the color A knotting cord.) Make an overhand knot on the tip of this cord to identify it.

Add Other Color Cords

5 Make an overhand knot with the other color knotting cords (according to the pattern), leaving a 2" (5cm) tail. Pin these cords to the board close to the mounted cords so they are ready when you need them **[c]**.

Make the Motifs

6 Each motif has 11 holding cords, and all the knots used on them are vertical DHHk except for the last row to finish the motifs. In the figures, each rectangle represents one vertical DHHk. Note that a vertical DHHk is longer than it is wide. Lengths for the knotting cords: one length for the diamond, twice the waves, twice the arrows, twice the abstract **[FIG 1–4]**.

Diamond Motif

I will guide you through the first rows of the diamond motif **[FIG 1]**. After that, follow the pattern using the tables as guides to complete this motif and then follow the patterns to complete the remaining motifs.

Row 1

This row runs left to right, so the knots are all vertical right-sided DHHk.

7 Number the holding cords from from 1–11, from left to right. Remember the second cord on the left with an over-hand knot on the tip is the color A knotting cord.

8 Using the color A knotting cord, make four vertical DHHk toward the right using cords 1–4 as holding cords **[d]**.

9 Set aside holding cords 6–11. Place the other color knotting cords under the leftmost five holding cords. (All of the knotting cords are now together **[e]**.)

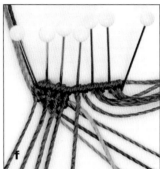

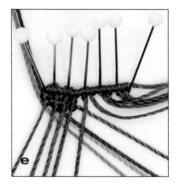

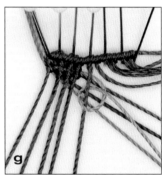

Before starting a new row, place the holding cords aside and pick them up one-by-one as needed to make the vertical DHHk. Do this so the cords will not get confused with the knotting cords. After you work on them, you can leave the cords hanging vertically while you finish the row.

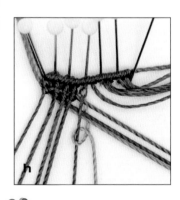

10 Carrying the knotting cords: Place the color B knotting cord on top of the other knotting cords **[f]**, and tie a half-hitch over holding cord 5, according to the pattern **[g]**. Pass the end of knotting cord B under the rest of the knotting cords, and then tie the other half-hitch over cord 5 **[h, FIG 5]**. Place the knotting cords in a horizontal or diagonal position while carrying the knotting cords to the right place.

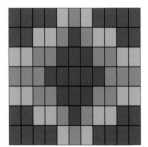
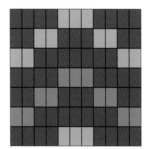

FIG 1   **FIG 2**

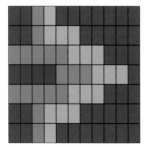
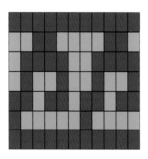

FIG 3   **FIG 4**

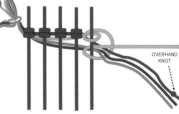

FIG 5

100

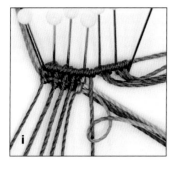

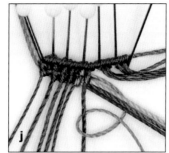

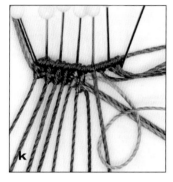

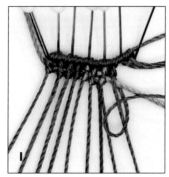

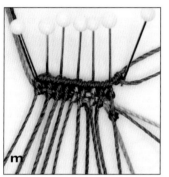

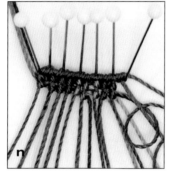

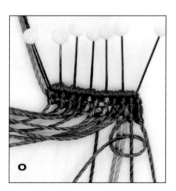

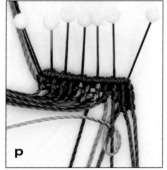

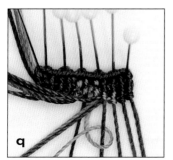

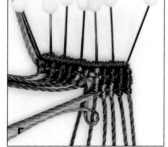

11 Place holding cord 6 over the knotting cords, and tie a vertical DHHk using the color C knotting cord. Carry the other three knotting cords as in step 10 **[i, j]**.

12 Using holding cord 7, and the color B knotting cord, tie a vertical DHHk over it. Carry the color A and C knotting cords only. Leave the color D knotting cord because you will need it here to make this color knot on the next row **[k]**. The knots may look loose, but they can be adjusted as you knot the following rows and later on at the end of the pattern.

13 Make the next four vertical DHHk (with holding cords 8–11) using the color A knotting cord. When you tie over cord 8, carry the color B and C knotting cords. **[l]**. Tie the knot over cord 9, carrying the color B knotting cord only **[m]**. Finally, tie over cords 10 and 11 without carrying any of the knotting cords. This completes the first row **[n]**.

Row 2
This row runs from right to left so all the knots are left-sided vertical DHHk. The knotting cords on this row are carried toward the left.

14 Start the row by placing the holding cords aside to the left except for holding cord 11. Following the pattern, bring back the color A knotting cord to the left by tying two vertical DHHk toward the leftover holding cords 10 and 11 **[o]**.

15 Using the color B knotting cord, make a vertical DHHk over holding cord 9. Carry the color A knotting cord **[p]**.

16 Using the same knotting cord (B), tie a vertical DHHk over holding cord 8. Carry the colors A and C knotting cords **[q]**.

17 Using the color C knotting cord, create a vertical DHHk over holding cord 7. Carry the color A and B knotting cords **[r]**.

18 Tie a vertical DHHk over holding cord 6, using the color D knotting cord. Carry to the left the rest of the knotting cords (A, B, and C) **[s, p. 102]**.

19 Make a vertical DHHk over holding cord 5 using the color C knotting cord. Carry the rest of the knotting cords (A, B, and D) **[t, p. 102]**.

Sparkling Waves *Earrings*

In this intricate design you will be using only vertical double half-hitch knots that go back and forth over two sets of holding cords. The changing number of knots on them result in the curved shape that is the focal point of the piece. The wavy motifs that form to the right make up the round shape of the earrings. They have dangling beads in the center that catch the eye and bring out the creative design of the knotted work.

MATERIALS & TOOLS

- 0.5mm nylon cords
  - **4** 40" (1.01m)
  - **2** 105" (2.67m)
- **2** 12mm round beads
- **4** 8° metal seed beads
- pair of earring wires
- embroidery needle
- superglue
- fabric glue
- **2** safety pins or paper clips
- scissors
- macramé board and pins

Material notes

Use nylon cord such as C-Lon beading cord, or S-Lon cord #18. These round beads are 12mm vintage-style sparkle balls with aurora borealis stones and a metal base.

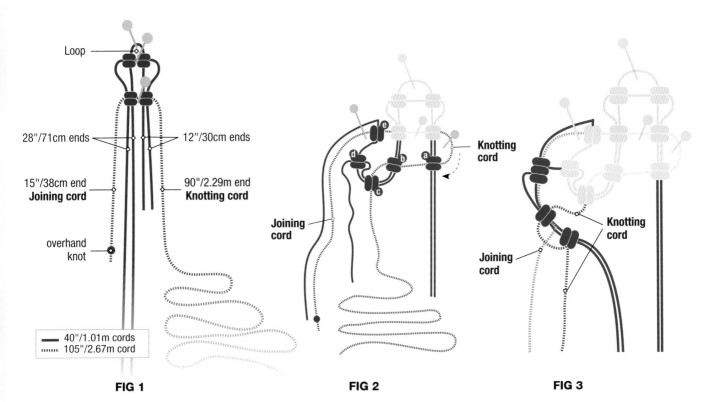

Loop

28"/71cm ends

12"/30cm ends

15"/38cm end
Joining cord

90"/2.29m end
Knotting cord

overhand
knot

Knotting
cord

Joining
cord

Knotting
cord

Joining
cord

— 40"/1.01m cords
······ 105"/2.67m cord

FIG 1

FIG 2

FIG 3

Mount the Cords

1 Refer to **FIG 1**: Place a pin on the board, and then lay one of the 40" (1m) threads on top of it so the left end is 28" (71cm). Tape the cord's right end to the board to hold it while you knot over its left end.

2 Using the other 40" cord and leaving 28" to the left, tie a vertical double half-hitch knot (DHHk) over the left end of the first cord **[a]**. Then, switching the tape to the left end, make another vertical DHHk over the right end **[b]**.

3 Slide the knots close to the pin, but leave a small loop (about 2mm) onto the first cord. Place a safety pin or a paper clip in the loop to prevent it from closing when you make adjustments. Make two pairs out of the cords. These will be the left and right holding cords throughout the work.

4 Place a pin in the middle of the cords to prevent the knots from sliding. Using a 105" (2.67m) cord, leave 15" (38cm) to the left and make a vertical DHHk over each pair of cords **[c]**. The short end of this cord is the joining cord, and it won't be used very often. Make an overhand knot on the tip of the joining cord to identify it. The long end is the knotting cord.

The First Motif

The first and last motifs are smaller and made differently than the rest.

5 Refer to **FIG 2**: Set the joining cord aside. Pass the knotting cord to the left under the right pair of cords, and tie a left-sided DHHk over them **(point a) [d]**. Over the left holding cords, make a left-sided DHHk **(point b)** and a right-sided DHHk **(point c)**. Release the knotting cord **[e]**.

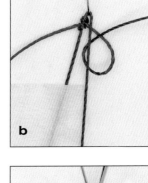

a

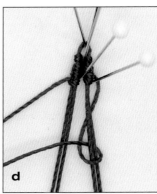

b

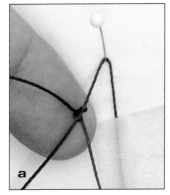

c

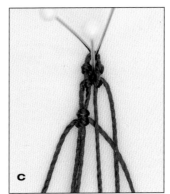

d

e

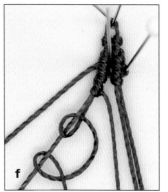

f

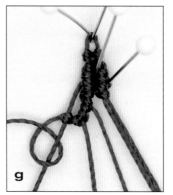

g

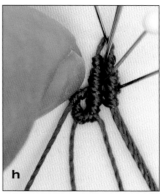

h

i

j

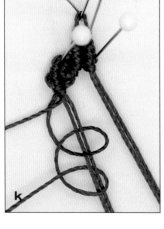

k

6 Using one of the holding cords, tie a right-sided DHHk **(point d)** over the other holding cord **[f]**. Of these two cords, always use the longer one so they are evenly used throughout the work. Use the remaining holding cord from the previous step as the knotting cord to tie a left-sided DHHk over the joining cord **(point e)**. Make this knot close to the previous knots **[g]**, then slide it with your thumbnail to form a curved shape **[h]**. Place a pin under the knot to keep it in place.

Finish the Motifs

Next, you will create a knotted line that surrounds motif 1 and motif 10 of the larger motifs in the same way.

7 Using the last knotting cord and the joining cord together as the holding cords, tie a triple half-hitch knot (THHk), using the next cord to the right **[i]**.

8 Refer to **FIG 3, p. 105**: Place the last knotting cord together with the previous holding cords for a total of three

holding cords, and make a DHHk using the knotting cord to the right **[j]**. Next, release the joining cord, passing it over the knotting cord. Remember, the joining cord is the cord with the overhand knot on its tip. Now, tie another DHHk in the same way and direction as the previous one **[k]**. This is the step where each motif ends. In the next step, you will keep using the same cords to make a knot in the opposite direction.

The Larger Motifs

Use the knotting cord to make a series of knots from left to right and vice versa over the left and right holding cords. There will be more knots on the left than on the right. This difference in the amount of knots will make the piece take a curved shape **[FIG 4]**. Then, create the larger motifs on the left side.

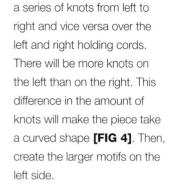

Joining cord

Knotting cord

FIG 4

9 Start from left to right. Use the knotting cord to make a THHk **(point a)** over the left holding cords **[l]** and a DHHk **(point b)** over the right holding cords. The knots on the right holding cords will be separated from the knots and positioned later.

To get the second knot (point b) close to the first one, place a pin to each side of the right holding cords, positioning them close to the first knot (point a). Tie the knot against the pins.

10 Bring the knotting cord back to the left. Place a pin to the left of the knotting cord, and tie a half-hitch **(point c)** on the right holding cords and then a DHHk **(point d)** on the left holding cords.

11 Returning to the right, create one DHHk **(points e and f)** over each pair of holding cords.

12 Bring the knotting cord back to the left. Place a pin to the left of the knotting cord, and tie a half-hitch **(point g)** on the right holding cords, then make a THHk **(point h)** **[m]** and a right-sided DHHk **(point i)** on the left holding cords. Release the knotting cord. The direction the knots are heading determines if they are right-sided or left-sided. In this case, on the left holding cords, the THHk is a left-sided

knot because it is heading to the left.

13 Next, take one of the holding cords to tie another right-sided DHHk **(point j)** over the other holding cord **[n]**.

14 Use the remaining holding cord from the previous step as the knotting cord to tie a left-sided DHHk **(point k)** over the joining cord. Make this knot close to the previous knots, and then slide it with your thumbnail to form a curved shape. Place a pin under the knot to keep it in place.

15 Pull the right holding cords to arrange the knots close together. Pulling the cords will make the piece take the curved shape. You are shaping the piece by pulling the right holding cords **[o]**.

16 Finish the motif by repeating steps 7 and 8. Use **FIG 3** as a guide **[p]**.

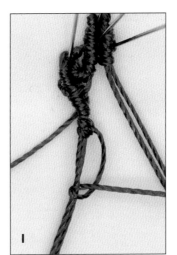

l

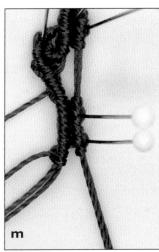

m

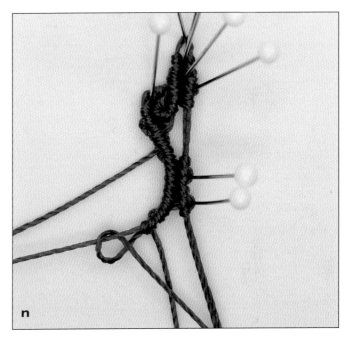

n

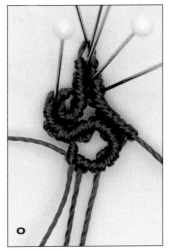

o

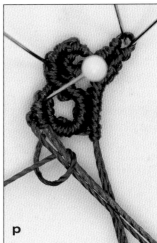

p

17 Repeat steps 6–16 **[q]** for a total of 10 larger motifs. Use **FIG 3** and **FIG 4** as a guide.

18 Make motif 11 following steps 9–15 only **[FIG 4]**. Then create a knotted line surrounding the motif as follows: As in step 7, take the last knotting cord and the joining cord together as the holding cords and tie a THHk, using the next cord to the right. Place the last knotting cord together with the previous holding cords for a total of three holding cords. Over these three holding cords, make a left-sided and a right-sided DHHk using the knotting cord that is to the right. Release the joining cord **[r]**. (You will continue knotting over the same (left) holding cords.)

Last Motif

19 Refer to **FIG 5**: Take the knotting cord to make a right-sided DHHk **(point a)** over the left holding cords and another DHHk **(point b)** over the right holding cords.

20 Bring the knotting cord back to the left. Place a pin to the left of the knotting cord, and tie a half-hitch **(point c)** on the right holding cords and then two alternating DHHk **(points d and e)** on the left holding cords, which will make the knotting cord end to the right. Release the knotting cord.

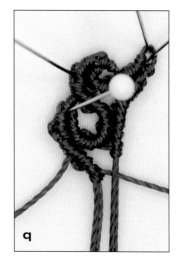

21 Next, take one of the holding cords to tie a right-sided DHHk **(point f)** over the other holding cord. Use the remaining holding cord from the previous step as the knotting cord to tie a left-sided DHHk **(point g)** over the joining cord **[s]**. Place a pin under the knot to keep it in place.

22 As in step 7, take the last knotting cord and the joining cord together as the holding cords and tie a THHk, using the next cord to the right **(point h)**. Place the last knotting cord together with the previous holding cords for a total of three holding cords. Starting with a left-sided knot, make two alternating DHHk using the knotting cord that is to the right **(points I and j)**. Do not release the joining cord.

23 Tie another DHHk over the right holding cords **(point k)**. Bring the knotting cord back to the left, making a DHHk over each, the right and left holding cords **(points l and m) [t]**.

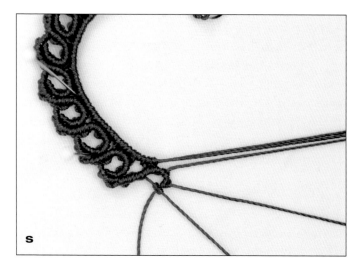

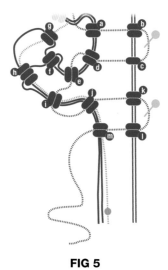

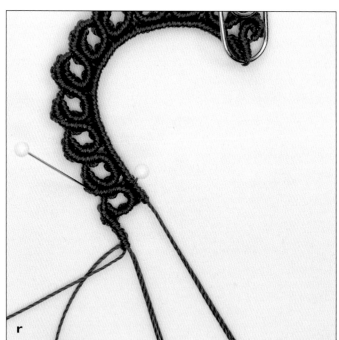

FIG 5

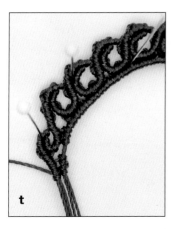

t

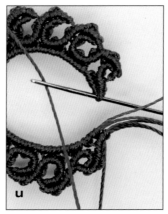

u

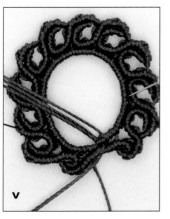

v

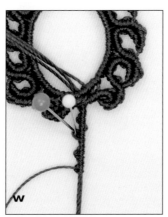

w

x

y

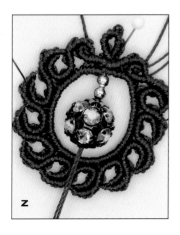

z

24 Repeat steps 1–24 to make an almost-completed second earring so that you can adjust them at the same time.

Finishing

25 Without removing the safety pins or paper clips, adjust and shape the earrings, arranging the knots on the right holding cords. Make sure both earrings look the same in shape and size. When you are happy with the way the pieces look, remove the paper clip or safety pin from the loop.

26 Set aside the knotting cord and with the help of an embroidery needle, pass the rest of the cords through the loop from the front to the back **[u]**. Trim the overhand knot on the joining cord.

27 Set aside three more cords. Later, two of them will be used to string the beads in the center of the earrings.

28 Use the knotting cord—which should be on the back of the piece—to tie a chain of four alternating DHHk over the remaining two cords **[v]**. Start with a right-sided DHHk.

29 Place two pins to the left of the chain to create a loop, and continue tying four more alternating DHHk **[w]**.

30 Thread the two holding cords through an embroidery needle, and pass them through the part where the piece comes together. The alternating DHHk chain will form a loop. Make sure the smaller loop in this chain is in the center **[x]**.

31 Leaving two cords in the center of the earring, secure the four remaining cords on the back of the piece. Thread the cords onto an embroidery needle, and pass them through the knots on the back of the work. Apply fabric glue to the knots where the cords have passed through to secure them **[y]**. Let the glue dry, and then and cut off the excess cords.

32 Using the two leftover cords, string the beads of your choice **[z]**. Make sure the beads move freely, and tie an overhand knot under the last bead. Apply a small dab of superglue over the knot, and trim the excess cord. Pass the earring wires through the small loop created in step 29.

Acknowledgments

Thanks to the people that have been involved in the process of writing this book:

Scott Saalman and Martine Callahan for their encouragement and for their wonderful help in writing my book's proposal.

My daughter Chantal for her invaluable help, assistance, and countless hours working side by side.

Margaret Garner, who taught me some lessons on proofreading and testing the projects, for her constant interest in my work, and for keeping in touch all of the time.

Mary Wohlgemuth, my editor for finding my work interesting and encouraging me to write the book. Without her, there would be no book.

These people for their support: My sister Celia, Dawn Standera, Arantxa Rodriguez, and MaJesus Villalonga

Marion Hunziker-Larsen, who taught me how to take care of the pieces.

Finally, thanks to all of my wonderful testers for their feedback.

about the author

Raquel Cruz is a passionate macramé artist, a graphic designer, and the author of several micro-macramé tutorials.

She learned macramé through an art class in middle school. Never knowing that jewelry, other than friendship bracelets, could be made using the technique, she came across a book on micro-macramé at a local library and from that day on, she has been using this technique that she had almost forgotten.

Raquel's experience with micro-macramé has turned her into an authoritative figure for this field of jewelry design. She has several tutorials currently appearing on Etsy.com. User feedback has been positive, which has inspired her to pursue publishing an actual book on her specialty art.

Thanks to continuous suggestions and petitions from people interested to know how she completed her projects, she began to use her knowledge as a graphic designer and micro-macramé knotter to put together tutorials like the ones found in this book.

Create More *Fun* and *Fashionable* Jewelry!

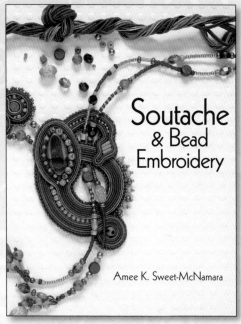

Soutache
& Bead
Embroidery

Amee K. Sweet-McNamara

Bead enthusiasts, fiber artists, and jewelry makers are falling in love with soutache. Bursting with vibrant color, this versatile cording introduces an intriguing fiber element to jewelry making. *Soutache & Bead Embroidery* offers you **18 projects** using this fresh technique – with no expensive materials or equipment required!
67507 ▪ $21.99

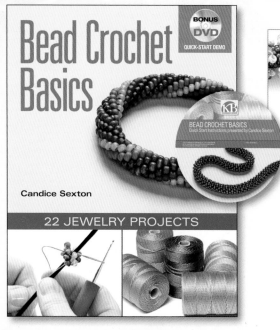

Bead Crochet
Basics

BONUS DVD
QUICK-START DEMO

Candice Sexton

22 JEWELRY PROJECTS

In *Bead Crochet Basics*, Candice Sexton takes the guesswork out of the trickiest part of bead crochet: starting the tube. Use the **included quick-start DVD** to see the setup in action, then progress through the 10 techniques and 22 projects with the confidence you need to succeed. Every jewelry maker will find something to make, wear, or share!
#64469 ▪ $21.99